Read and Think!

A Reading Strategies Course

PEARSON

Longman

Published by
Longman Asia ELT
2/F Cornwall House
Taikoo Place
979 King's Road
Quarry Bay
Hong Kong

fax: +852 2856 9578
email: pearsonlongman@pearsoned.com.hk
www.longman.com

and Associated Companies throughout the world.

First published 2004
Reprinted 2006
Produced by Pearson Education Asia Limited, Hong Kong
GCC/04

ISBN-13: 978-962-01-8399-7
ISBN-10: 962-01-8399-1

Design Manager: Winnie Sung
Editors: Gregg Schroeder, Mark Horsley
Designer: Waimann Lee
Illustrators: Brian Wan, Waimann Lee

Thanks to Audio Producer David Pope and Sky Productions; voice artists Derrick Stone, Melissa Nesbitt, Sheri Dorfman, Arvin Robles, Jovelyn Fuego and Ken Beatty.

We are grateful to Corbis for permission to reproduce copyright photographs.

Author acknowledgments
A great many people worked hard to make this book a success, including all those who gave suggestions on early drafts and outlines. Great thanks go to my meticulous and creative editor Gregg Schroeder for thoughtful drudgery during weekends and late nights, to Mark Horsley for editorial support and to Waimann Lee, who organized words into visual ideas.

Thanks also to my colleague at City University of Hong Kong, Nicola Gram, for her help.

As always, I thank my wife Ann for unceasing support and beg forgiveness of my sons, Nathan and Spencer, for lost play.

Introduction to students

Getting the most out of *Read and Think!*

Do you like to read? Would you like to read better?

Reading is more than just knowing a lot of words. When you read different kinds of texts, you need to know what strategies and skills to use. You also need to have a basic knowledge of different disciplines, such as university subjects.

Read and Think! is a four-level series to help you improve your reading. It's made up of many different parts. Each unit is divided into two lessons. Each lesson features an interesting reading passage. The passages included are presented as articles, movie reviews, letters, plays, poems, speeches and stories.

The two passages in each unit give two points of view on the same topic. The topics are followed by different kinds of exercises, such as fill-in-the-blanks, multiple choice, matching and short answer. Once you've finished the unit, you have a chance to show what you know by discussing debate topics.

Reading is not just a skill for words, but also for images. So, to make the book more interesting for you, cartoons, charts, diagrams, illustrations, maps and photos are included, with activities to help you think.

Throughout each unit, help in the form of *Reading strategies, Language notes, Exam strategies, Debate strategies, Computer notes* and *Culture notes* is provided. Special *Concepts* boxes expand on core ideas within readings and *What about you?* sections let you think about how the topic of the unit relates to you.

Beyond the book, topics for further study and online resources are included on the companion website. Your teacher can also help you measure what you learn by using photocopied quizzes.

Reading is a lifetime skill—learn to do it well!

Ken Beatty

Introduction to teachers

Working with *Read and Think!*

Read and Think! is written by a teacher for teachers. The purpose of the four-level series is to help your students see reading as an interesting problem-solving activity. The series improves students' reading skills while covering issues important to students, including ethical and academic issues. These issues are presented in a variety of text types with carefully integrated graphics.

The four Student Books each offer twelve units. Each unit is divided into two lessons.

Level 1: 250–300 words per reading
Level 2: 300–400 words per reading
Level 3: 600–700 words per reading
Level 4: 800+ words per reading

Unit content
Each unit begins with a title and key words taken from general areas of knowledge, usually university disciplines.

Lesson One
- **Before you read** starts off with questions to make students think about the new topic. Ask students to discuss the questions in pairs or small groups or use them as a whole-class activity. A picture, map, diagram or illustration follows with something for the students to do. Use this to create more interest in the topic and explore new vocabulary.
- **Read about it** takes students into the first of the unit's two main readings. After listening, students read on their own. Finally, students read and listen together to match pronunciation with comprehension. Key vocabulary notes from the *Longman Dictionary of Contemporary English* help students learn key words, and space at the back of the book is provided for students to write their own dictionary, adding unfamiliar words as they encounter them.
- **After you read** gives students a chance to show what they know by asking questions about the reading. An *Understand what you read* section on understanding what they read helps to explain a key point of learning English. The *What about you?* section helps students see their own place in the topic.

Lesson Two

- **Read about it** offers another perspective on the unit topic to help students think about what they read. Sometimes these second readings take the opposite point of view. Start off by listening to get the students involved. Ask students to listen with their books closed.
- **After you read** has a higher level task, such as summarizing a paragraph in one sentence, as well as fun activities, including word puzzles. This is followed by multiple choice comprehension questions.
- **Debate** gives students a chance to show what they know based on arguing a point made in the unit. Two perspectives on the same idea are given with supporting points and room for students to add their own ideas.

Strategies and *notes* help students with reading, language, culture and exams, and are found throughout the unit.

Other **Read and Think!** components include:
- Teacher's Manual, with teaching notes and answer keys
- CD of all passages
- CD-ROM Test Bank, which can be used to produce photocopy masters
- Website at **www.read-and-think.com**, with teacher and student support

Contents

Are You a Genius?

Lesson One

Before you read

- What is a genius?
- Who are some famous geniuses?

Label the pictures.

helicopter	giant crossbow	crossbow machine	tank

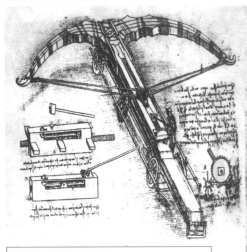

a.

b.

c.

d.

Reading strategy

Reading a picture is just like reading a passage. Look for the main idea. In a photograph, it's often whatever is at the center of the picture. In a drawing, it's often the part with the most detail.

- Listen for words from other languages.

Leonardo da Vinci

Leonardo da Vinci, self-portait

Leonardo da Vinci was born on April 15, 1452, to a young woman named Caterina, who may have been one of his father's servants. Leonardo's father, Ser Piero, lived in Vinci, a small town close to the city of Florence, in what is now Italy. The name of the town gave Leonardo his last name: the *da* in *da Vinci* means *of*. Ser Piero was a wealthy notary.

As his parents were not married, Leonardo lived the first five years of his life with his mother in another town. When she married someone else, Leonardo was sent to live with his father's ever-growing family. Leonardo's father married four times in his long life and eventually had eighteen children!

Because Ser Piero was educated and wealthy, he had something valuable that most people never even had a chance to touch: books. In Europe, printing wasn't invented until the mid-fifteenth century and so most people did not have books. Up to that time, books were made by hand, usually copied out on expensive sheep skin. As for school, Leonardo only took a few lessons from a local priest but never had a proper education.

So how did Leonardo come to be regarded as one of the greatest geniuses of all time? There are probably at least six factors.

2

The first and saddest reason may simply have been a need to belong. Leonardo was born without a proper father in his home and, when he was five, his mother left, and possibly never saw him again. It must have been difficult for a young child. Perhaps Leonardo's attempts to understand the world grew from trying to understand why he had been abandoned. | 30

Second, Leonardo had the opportunity to observe creative people. His hometown of Vinci was famous for its many painting workshops. As a child, Leonardo probably wandered the streets and sat watching local artists painting in their studios. | 35

Third, Leonardo was fascinated with nature. One of his earliest memories was of a bird waking him in his bed. When he was young, Leonardo roamed the countryside around Vinci and seems to have taken a great interest in everything around him: insects, plants, animals, natural features, bodies of water and the weather. His interest in nature continued throughout his life. | 40

Fourth, Leonardo developed systematic skills for looking at and recording his world. Contemporary accounts suggest that when he was a child, he was already skillful as a painter. One particular story told about him says that he was asked to draw a decoration on a battle shield. Leonardo decided to paint a fearsome Medusa head: a woman with snakes | 45 for hair whose glance could turn a person to stone. Leonardo collected not only snakes but also lizards and various insects and drew them until the stench drove everyone from his room. He did not notice, but merely concentrated on his painting. In the end, it was so good, his father decided to sell it rather than give it to the man who had asked for it.

Fifth, Leonardo was born at a time of | 55 exciting change and opportunity. Europe in the fifteenth century began what is called a *renaissance,* or rebirth, during which the ancient

Medusa, by Caravaggio

Reading strategy

Authors often introduce numbered lists in their writing. Sometimes they use numerals *1, 2, 3*, etc., and other times they use ordinal numbers, *first, second, third* and so on. Make sure you understand each point before going on to the next one.

writings of Greek and Roman thinkers, as well as those of Muslim academics,
were re-examined. Both science and art flourished, especially as wealthy
patrons were willing to pay artists and thinkers to create new ideas. When he
was eight, Leonardo moved to Florence. It was one of the wealthiest and most
interesting cities in the world at that time, under the control of the Medici
family, international bankers who had the largest library in Europe. When
he was fifteen, Leonardo was apprenticed to a famous artist whose studio
made everything from decorations to paintings to sculpture.

Finally, Leonardo wrote about and drew what he learned. His advice, which
you should follow, is: "With slight strokes, take a note in a little book which
you should always carry with you."

(644 words)

Vocabulary notes

1. **abandon** (verb) to leave someone, especially someone you are responsible for
2. **apprentice** (verb) to work for an employer for a fixed period of time in order to learn a particular skill or job
3. **factor** (noun) one of several things that influence or cause a situation
4. **invent** (verb) to make, design, or think of a new type of thing
5. **notary** (noun) someone, especially a lawyer, who has the legal power to make a signed statement or document official
6. **proper** (adjective) right, suitable or correct
7. **roam** (verb) to walk or travel, usually for a long time, with no clear purpose or direction
8. **shield** (noun) a large piece of metal or leather that soldiers used in the past to protect themselves when fighting
9. **systematic** (adjective) organized carefully and done thoroughly
10. **studio** (noun) a room where a painter or a photographer regularly works

Add new words to your personal dictionary on page 176.

Read and listen again to practice your pronunciation.

After you read

A. Answer these questions.

1. Why might young Leonardo have felt he did not belong?
2. How did Leonardo learn about nature?
3. What advice did Leonardo have for others?
4. When did Leonardo move to Florence?
5. Who did Leonardo observe to learn about art?

Understand what you read

Foreign words

Foreign words are often used in English for a variety of reasons. The first reason is to use original place names: *Firenze*, for example, may be used instead of its English version, *Florence*. Another reason is for concepts that are not easily translated into English or which are more common in their original language. Often, foreign words are used for humor.

Here are four tips for dealing with foreign words:

- Try to understand the reason why the author has included the foreign word.
- Foreign words are often set in *italics*.
- Countless foreign words, from *pajamas* (Indian) to *café* (French), have become English words and are not set in italics.
- Decide whether the foreign word you read is useful and should be memorized.

Computer note

Many foreign words will be identified as possible misspellings by word processor spell checks. Double check them.

B. Read these sentences and decide the meaning of the foreign words by context.

1. The Moroccan *tagine* is made by cooking chicken pieces with vegetables and dried fruit for several hours.
2. The Russian ambassador absolutely disagreed; she said *nyet* to everything!
3. It's hard to truly understand beauty; it has a certain *je ne sais quoi*.
4. Many people think it's cruel to go to a bull ring just to see a *matador* show his skill.
5. He didn't want to argue, so he pleaded *nolo contendo* before the judge.

Reading strategy

Most foreign words can be understood by context. Read ahead and see if they become clear. If not, go back and look up the word or expression later. If it's not in your dictionary, try the WWW.

C. What do you know?

To go from being an apprentice to a master, Leonardo had to paint a *masterpiece*. Now all of his fifteen remaining paintings are considered masterpieces. How many can you name?

D. Fill in the missing words. Use the correct form of the word.

- **downfall** (noun) complete loss of your money, moral standards, social position, etc., or the sudden failure of an organization
- **experiment** (verb) to try using various ideas, methods, etc., to find out how good or effective they are
- **innovate** (verb) to start to use new ideas, methods or inventions
- **masterpiece** (noun) a work of art, a piece of writing or music, etc., that is of very high quality or that is the best that a particular artist, writer, etc., has produced
- **technique** (noun) a special way of doing something

Reading strategy

Remember that titles of artwork and the names of books are usually set in *italics*.

A great deal of Leonardo's genius lay in the fact that he was always _____ innovating _____ . But it was also his _____ . He was never satisfied to do things the way they were done before so he _____ with new _____ in painting and sculpture. One of his most famous _____ , *The Last Supper*, began to decay almost as soon as he finished it.

What inventions made Leonardo da Vinci famous?

What about you?

You might want to join Mensa if you're a genius. To join, you need to pass some intelligence tests. Start with these three simple questions:

1. Write the next number in the sequence. 3, 5, 8, 13, _____
2. Write the next set of letters in the sequence: bat, cet, dit, fot, _____
3. An American plane carrying Canadian passengers crashes in Mexico and 212 people are killed. Where are the survivors buried?

Answers
1. 21: the numbers are additive; each new number is the sum of the previous two.
2. **gut**: based on the order of the consonants and vowels in the English alphabet.
3. Nowhere. You don't bury survivors.

Lesson Two

- What is Albert Einstein famous for?
- How does Albert Einstein's childhood differ from Leonardo da Vinci's? How is it similar?

Albert Einstein

Albert Einstein was born on March 14, 1879, in Ulm, Germany. His parents were Hermann and Pauline Einstein. Albert's father was an accountant but he was also a businessman, working with his brother, Jacob. Jacob Einstein was an inventor and together the Einstein brothers invented and sold a variety of electrical equipment. At this time, electric lights were just starting to replace gas lights.

As a child, Albert was a considerable worry to his parents: he did not speak. In fact, he did not begin to talk until he reached the age of three. As the story goes, he finally spoke at a family dinner one night, skipping over baby language and astounding everyone with a fully-formed sentence,

Albert Einstein, aged about eight, with his sister, Maja, ca. 1884

"The soup is too hot."

When asked why he had not spoken before, he replied, "Because up to now, everything was in order." After this first discussion, Albert still did not like to talk a great deal. Nor did he like to play with other children. Instead, like many children, he took his toys extremely seriously and would play with them endlessly, trying to understand exactly how they worked.

Albert's shyness did not extend to adults, if he wanted to know the answers to questions. And he had many questions. Typical of these were questions about gravity. Why, for example, does a leaf fall down while the moon stays suspended in the sky?

He was fortunate that his parents and uncle were scientifically minded and were able to help answer his questions. Many other parents—and teachers—would have laughed and ignored him.

A real turning point in Albert's "education" happened when he was five. He fell sick and was confined to bed. During this time, his father gave him a present that was to fascinate him as much as his question about the moon: a magnetic compass. Albert struggled to understand why its needle always pointed north.

In 1885, Albert started school but immediately hated it. Under the German system of the time, the teachers could punish wrong answers with beatings. The classes were generally boring with students forced to memorize and repeat exactly what their teachers said. Fortunately, Albert excelled in science and mathematics because of his natural interest in these subjects, but other subjects were difficult for him. His teachers had few hopes he would ever amount to anything.

Einstein in later years

Outside of school, Albert discovered other interests: sailing and music. He joked that sailing was a wonderful sport because it required so little energy. As for music, his mother played piano and encouraged Albert to take up the violin. He enjoyed playing the violin for the rest of his life, although he wasn't the best player. Albert often played with other mathematicians and physicists in small groups, but one fellow musician complained about him. When playing music with others, it's necessary to count the beats of the music to stay in time with each other. Einstein—the most famous mathematician of all time—couldn't count!

Another turning point in Albert's education was his introduction to a young medical student, Max Talmey. It was the custom for families to help out university students by inviting them for dinner, and Max was a frequent visitor to the Einstein home. Albert always had many questions for Max about mathematics and science, and Max began supplying Albert with advanced textbooks on these subjects. By the time he was twelve,

110 Albert knew much more than Max and more than most math teachers.

By the time he was sixteen, Albert had begun to ask questions about the nature of light and gravity. Answering those 115 questions would lead him to the Nobel Prize as well as ideas that made possible the creation of the atomic bomb.

(622 words)

Underwater test of an atomic bomb in the Marshall Islands, 1946

Vocabulary notes

1. **accountant** (noun) someone whose job is to keep and check financial accounts, calculate taxes, etc.
2. **astound** (verb) to make someone very surprised or shocked
3. **confined** (adjective) if you are confined to a place, you have to stay in that place, especially because you are ill
4. **excel** (verb) to do something very well, or much better than most people
5. **gravity** (noun) the force that causes something to fall to the ground or to be attracted to another planet
6. **Nobel Prize** (noun) one of the prizes given each year to people who have done important work in various types of activity. There are prizes for special achievements in physics, chemistry, economics, literature and peace. The Nobel Prizes were established by Alfred Nobel and are given in Sweden. It is a great honor to receive a Nobel Prize, and people who have received them are called Nobel laureates.
7. **shyness** (noun) the state of being nervous and embarrassed about meeting and speaking to other people, especially people you do not know
8. **turning point** (noun) the time when an important change starts, especially one that improves the situation

Read and listen again to practice your pronunciation.

After you read

A. Summarize the main idea in one sentence.

In December 1932, Albert Einstein left his native Germany to visit the United States. Soon after, the Nazi Party under Adolph Hitler came to power in Germany and began to persecute Jews, including Einstein. As part of this persecution, 100 Nazi professors published a book criticizing Einstein's key theory, the Theory of Relativity. Einstein thought this was amusing and said, "If I were wrong, one professor would have been enough."

B. Vocabulary check: Fill in the missing letters to find the secert word.

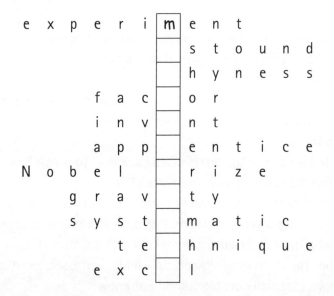

C. Choose the best answer.

1. Leonardo's last name came from the name of ___ .
   a. a fearsome head
   b. a wealthy family in Florence
   c. an academic during the Renaissance
   d. the town where his father lived

2. Books in the fifteenth century ___ .
   a. were few and expensive
   b. were not useful
   c. did not exist
   d. were only read by geniuses

3. Leonardo's genius was not a result of his ___ .
   a. need to belong
   b. parents' support
   c. interest in nature
   d. observational skills

4. Leonardo was *fascinated with* nature and *roamed* the countryside.
   a. enjoyed, studied about
   b. interested in, walked throughout
   c. moved by, recorded
   d. motivated by, painted

5. Hermann Einstein was ___ .
   a. a student who worked with his brother
   b. a businessman who worked with his father
   c. an accountant who worked with his brother
   d. a salesman who worked with his father

6. Albert's parents worried because he ___ .
   a. asked many questions
   b. was very shy
   c. took his toys very seriously
   d. didn't speak until the age of three

7. Albert's answer to why he hadn't spoken suggests ___ .
   a. everything had been fine
   b. starting from then, things were disorganized
   c. before, everything was in disorder
   d. in the future, things will be more systematic

8. In line 55, quotation marks surround Albert's "education" because ___ .
   a. it was not formal education in school
   b. it was pre-school for young children
   c. his parents were not teachers
   d. he was not learning from books

9. Which is not a reason why Albert hated school?
   a. Teachers punished students for giving wrong answers.
   b. Classes were generally boring.
   c. Students were forced to memorize and repeat.
   d. Books were rare and expensive.

10. In line 74, *amount to anything* means ___ .
    a. be rich
    b. be successful
    c. be smart
    d. be popular

Exam strategy

In writing exams, don't try to make your writing too clever when you answer a question. Use direct simple sentences so you are sure the teacher knows what you mean.

Debate

Take one side, add your own ideas and debate in pairs or groups.

For: Everyone can be a genius at something.

Points:

- Genius is mostly applying yourself to a particular problem for a long time.

- Geniuses simply try to see familiar problems in new ways.

- Most breakthroughs occur in the mind, not in expensive laboratories.

- _____

- _____

- _____

Against: Geniuses are born, not made.

Points:

- Some people are simply far better at thinking about problems than others.

- Most major problems are now solved by well-trained scientists.

- If everyone were a genius, who would take out the garbage?

- _____

- _____

- _____

Debate strategy

When you debate, start your argument by introducing your point of view and summarizing your main points. You can also summarize your opponent's reasons and examples, then present your own.

Say:

- "I believe that ... for three reasons."
- "My opponent has said ... but the opposite is actually true for three reasons ... ."

More ideas to debate

"It's not that I'm so smart, it's just that I stay with problems longer."
Albert Einstein (1879–1955) Scientist

"Genius is another word for magic, and the whole point of magic is that it is inexplicable."
Margot Fonteyn (1919–1991) Dancer

"The secret of genius is to carry the spirit of childhood into maturity."
Thomas Henry Huxley (1825–1895) Scientist

"To see things in the seed, that is genius."
Lao-Tzu (570?–490? BC) Philosopher, founder of Taoism

Think about it

Margaret Fonteyn was considered a genius. But she wasn't a scientist. What did she do?

Learn more

Many people are called geniuses, sometimes in different fields, such as sports and music. Find examples of people who are geniuses and report about them to your class.

Look online

Check out the website at www.read-and-think.com for extra learning resources.

Add new words to your personal dictionary on page 176.

Your Rights?

Lesson One

Before you read

- What rights should everyone have?
- What are human rights?

What is happening in the picture?

Little Rock, Arkansas, USA, 1957

Photo tip

Photographs tell about moments. Most photographers take dozens of pictures on either side of their final choice. The best photograph is usually the one that tells the best story. What story does this photo tell?

Read about it

- Listen for the different kinds of rights.

Who—and What—Has Rights?

Do plants have rights? Some people think so. Fruitarians are people who think it is cruel to kill a plant just because you are hungry. Instead, they wait until the plant is dead or gives up some food in the form of fallen fruit. For example, a fruitarian will not pick an apple; he or she will wait until it has fallen onto the ground and then eat it.

Most people are not fruitarians; they are omnivores, people who eat all kinds of food. But still, some omnivores draw a line in terms of what they think they should eat based on their respect—or lack of respect—for the thing they are eating. For example, some people think it is cruel to eat wild animals, but are quite happy to eat wild fish. Many think it is not right to eat endangered animals, such as pandas, which may become extinct. Usually, there are laws to protect such animals. But for some people, breaking such laws only makes the animals more attractive as exotic meals. Others are against eating animals such as dogs and cats, but this is practiced throughout parts of Asia.

An endangered civet cat in Guangzhou, China

15

How about humans? Should people eat other humans? On this subject, most people and laws would agree that they should not, but being a cannibal has reportedly been common at different times throughout history. But why is it OK to eat a plant and not a human?

Cannibals supposedly cooked human body parts in the New World

Part of the answer probably lies in our belief that we should not kill other thinking, feeling animals. But people think different humans and animals have different rights. These rights are not just the right to life, but different rights of how they should be treated.

Human rights is a recent topic so people's beliefs vary greatly around the world. Slavery, the practice of owning people, is still common in parts of the world. In some Islamic countries, the rights of women are extremely limited. A woman is, as she was a century ago in Western countries, part of her husband's property. The right to go to school, to go out alone in public, to drive a car or to vote are all restricted in various countries. In some, a woman's place at home is fourth (after her husband, her son and the family camel). A woman who does the same work as a man may be paid much less. Are her rights being violated?

Freedom of expression is a hotly debated right. Some countries, such as the United States, see it as one of the most important rights. The First Amendment to the United States Constitution states that "Congress shall make no law ... abridging the freedom of speech ... or the right of the people ... to petition the government for a redress of grievances." However, other countries, such as Canada, limit that freedom and say that freedom of expression does not mean you can spread hate and lies.

China is one country that has often been criticized for its abuse of human rights, including freedom of expression. However, the Chinese government

Caged cattle, feeding

sees the issue differently. It ties human rights to development and notes that before 1949, 80 percent of its population lived in starvation or near-starvation. In 1946 alone, 10 million Chinese starved to death. Through tight government controls, China has raised the quality of life for the majority of its people. The right to quality of life, they argue, is more important than other rights. The government also argues that a stable society is more important than the individual rights of those who challenge the government.

What *is* certain is that different views on rights will continue to be debated.

(611 words)

Reading strategy

The author starts by asking about plants' rights, but the focus of the article goes onto another topic. When you are reading for comprehension, don't assume that the first sentence or first paragraph is the main point the author is making.

Vocabulary notes

1. **cannibal** (noun) someone who eats human flesh
2. **criticize** (verb) to express your disapproval of someone or something, or to talk about their faults
3. **exotic** (adjective) something that is exotic seems unusual and interesting because it is related to a foreign country—use this to show approval
4. **omnivore** (noun) an animal that eats both meat and plants
5. **respect** (noun) when you regard something or someone as important and are careful not to harm them, treat them rudely, etc.
6. **violate** (verb) to disobey or do something against an official agreement, law, principle, etc.

Add new words to your personal dictionary on page 176.

Read and listen again to practice your pronunciation.

After you read

A. Answer these questions.

1. Why might women's rights be restricted in some countries?
2. What does the article say about cannibalism?
3. Do the same rights apply to all living things?
4. What are two views on the freedom of expression?
5. How is China's view of rights different from other countries?

Understand what you read

Explanations in context

When you read, explanations of new or unusual words and phrases are often defined by the author in context. Most commonly, this is done by adding a short explanation in commas, after the word.

- *Human rights, or the right to be treated in a fair and equal way, usually include ... .*

Sometimes, the word is followed by an explanation in parentheses.

- *Slavery (keeping and selling people against their will) is illegal but still widespread.*

The word or phrase can be followed by a paraphrase, in which one or more words is changed to make the meaning clearer.

- *Freedom from fear, or freedom from being afraid of one's own government, is seldom present in a dictatorship.*

Here are three tips for reading explanations in context:

- Sometimes a writer gives a new definition of a word or phrase.
- Sometimes a writer emphasizes a particular definition of a word.
- The purpose of good writing is to communicate. If you cannot understand what you are reading, think of the reason. Is it because you do not have enough background knowledge? Is the vocabulary too difficult? Or are you reading for detail rather than for the general idea?

B. Find an example of each in the passage.

1. A short explanation in commas
2. An explanation in parentheses
3. A phrase followed by a paraphrase

C. Number the pictures 1 to 5 from the most rights to the least rights.

D. Fill in the missing words. Use the correct form of the word.

- **best interest** (noun) the best thing for someone
- **capable** (adjective) having the qualities or ability needed to do something
- **ethical** (adjective) relating to principles of what is right and wrong
- **experimentation** (noun) the process of testing various ideas, methods, etc., to find out how good or effective they are
- **suffering** (noun) serious physical or mental pain

People for the _____ Treatment of Animals (PETA) believes that animals deserve the most basic rights—consideration of their own _____ regardless of whether they are useful to humans. Like you, they are _____ of _____ and have interests in leading their own lives; therefore, they are not ours to use for food, clothing, entertainment, _____ —or for any other reason.

Source: PETA, www.peta.org

Reading strategy

Most organizations summarize their goals in a short mission statement explaining what they stand for. These are usually concise and easy to read.

What other organizations protect the rights of animals?

What about you?

What special rights do you think you should have? For example, should you have the right to drive a car when you're thirteen years old? Make a list.

Lesson Two

- This is an official document and is difficult to understand as it uses a lot of legal English. Don't try to understand every word. Listen to get the general idea, then skim to get the main idea of each paragraph.

Spirit of Brotherhood:
Universal Declaration of Human Rights

On December 10, 1948, the General Assembly of the United Nations adopted and proclaimed the Universal Declaration of Human Rights, a portion of which [5] appears below. Following this historic act, the Assembly called upon all Member countries to publicize the text of the Declaration and "to cause it to be disseminated, [10] displayed, read and expounded principally in schools and other educational institutions, without distinction based on the political status of countries or territories." [15]

PREAMBLE

Whereas recognition of the inherent dignity and of the equal and inalienable rights of all members of the human family is the [20]

United Nations Building, New York

foundation of freedom, justice and peace in the world,

Whereas disregard and contempt for human rights have resulted in barbarous acts which have outraged the conscience of mankind, and the advent of a world in which human beings shall enjoy freedom of speech and belief and freedom from fear and want has been proclaimed as the highest aspiration of the common people,

Whereas it is essential, if man is not to be compelled to have recourse, as a last resort, to rebellion against tyranny and oppression, that human rights should be protected by the rule of law,

Whereas it is essential to promote the development of friendly relations between nations,

Whereas the peoples of the United Nations have in the Charter reaffirmed their faith in fundamental human rights, in the dignity and worth of the human person and in the equal rights of men and women and have determined to promote social progress and better standards of life in larger freedom,

Whereas Member States have pledged themselves to achieve, in cooperation with the United Nations, the promotion of universal respect for and observance of human rights and fundamental freedoms,

Whereas a common understanding of these rights and freedoms is of the greatest importance for the full realization of this pledge,

Now, Therefore THE GENERAL ASSEMBLY proclaims THIS UNIVERSAL DECLARATION OF HUMAN RIGHTS as a common standard of achievement for all peoples and all nations, to the end that every individual and every organ of society, keeping this Declaration constantly in mind, shall strive by teaching and education to promote respect for these rights and freedoms and by progressive measures, national and international, to secure their universal and effective recognition and observance, both among the peoples of Member States themselves and among the peoples of territories under their jurisdiction.

Article 1.

All human beings are born free and equal in dignity and rights. They are endowed with reason and conscience and should act towards one another in a spirit of brotherhood.

Article 2.

Everyone is entitled to all the rights and freedoms set forth in this Declaration, without distinction of any kind, such as race, color, sex, language, religion, political or other opinion, national or social origin, property, birth or other status. Furthermore, no distinction shall be made on the basis of the political, jurisdictional or international status of the country or territory to which a person belongs, whether it be independent, trust, non-self-governing or under any other limitation of sovereignty.

Article 3.

Everyone has the right to life, liberty and security of person.

Article 4.

No one shall be held in slavery or servitude; slavery and the slave trade shall be prohibited in all their forms.

Article 5.

No one shall be subjected to torture or to cruel, inhuman or degrading treatment or punishment.

Article 6.

Everyone has the right to recognition everywhere as a person before the law.

Article 7.

All are equal before the law and are entitled without any discrimination to equal protection of the law. All are entitled to equal protection against any discrimination in violation of this Declaration and against any incitement to such discrimination.

(616 words)

Source: United Nations www.un.org

Vocabulary notes

1. **fundamental** (adjective) relating to the most basic and important parts of something
2. **inalienable** (adjective) an inalienable right, power, etc., cannot be taken from you
3. **incite** (verb) to deliberately encourage people to fight, argue, etc., —incitement (noun)
4. **oppression** (noun) when someone treats a group of people unfairly or cruelly and prevents them from having the same rights as other people have
5. **preamble** (noun) a statement at the beginning of a book, document or talk, explaining what it is about
6. **proclaim** (verb) to say publicly or officially that something important is true or exists
7. **torture** (noun) an act of deliberately hurting someone in order to force them to tell you something, to punish them, or to be cruel
8. **tyranny** (noun) cruel or unfair control over other people
9. **whereas** (conjugation) used to say that although something is true of one thing, it is not true of another

Read and listen again to practice your pronunciation.

22

After you read

A. Summarize the main idea in one sentence.

Article 26.

(1) Everyone has the right to education. Education shall be free, at least in the elementary and fundamental stages. Elementary education shall be compulsory. Technical and professional education shall be made generally available and higher education shall be equally accessible to all on the basis of merit.

B. Vocabulary check: Circle the words.

C	W	E	X	Z	C	W	R	D	T	V	C	T	V	C	T
A	T	Y	G	F	F	Z	M	C	F	C	U	P	L	O	B
P	J	M	S	F	H	A	H	A	L	X	C	R	I	M	Z
A	T	E	U	O	R	F	F	N	I	N	R	O	N	N	V
B	Y	T	F	P	E	C	U	N	C	P	I	C	C	I	I
L	R	H	F	P	S	T	N	I	E	R	T	L	I	V	O
E	A	I	E	R	P	O	D	B	N	E	I	A	T	O	L
X	N	C	R	E	E	R	A	A	S	A	C	I	E	R	A
P	N	A	I	S	C	T	M	L	E	M	I	M	M	E	T
C	Y	L	N	S	T	U	E	I	B	B	Z	E	E	S	E
H	B	R	G	I	G	R	N	S	Z	L	E	D	N	O	D
E	F	S	O	O	O	E	T	M	T	E	M	P	T	P	W
Z	D	O	U	N	L	G	A	D	X	E	X	O	T	I	C
G	M	A	Q	S	F	J	L	C	Q	G	R	J	C	F	A
I	N	A	L	I	E	N	A	B	L	E	H	U	G	T	U
E	X	P	E	R	I	M	E	N	T	A	T	I	O	N	T

fundamental	preamble	cannibal	respect	experimentation
inalienable	proclaim	criticize	violate	suffering
incite	torture	exotic	capable	
oppression	tyranny	omnivore	ethical ✔	

C. Choose the best answer.

1. Fruitarians believe that ___ .
   a. plants are hungry
   b. plants are generous
   c. plants can eat, too
   d. plants can feel

2. *Cannibalism* means humans ___ .
   a. eating fruit and plants
   b. eating omnivores
   c. eating humans
   d. eating animals

3. Line 12 in the first passage is an example of ___ .
   a. an animal's right
   b. an explanation in context
   c. a goal
   d. legal English

4. The quote from the First Amendment to the United States Constitution means that ___ .
   a. all should have the right to be free; this includes the right to speak freely
   b. disagreement should be defended to the death
   c. the right to debate is the most important right
   d. freedom of expression is more important than the content of the expression

5. China's policy toward human rights can be summed up as:
   a. Human rights are more important than freedom of expression.
   b. Government rights are more important than individual rights.
   c. Other rights are more important than the right to quality of life.
   d. Group rights are more important than individual rights.

6. In lines 13–14 in the second passage, *without distinction* means ___ .
   a. nothing special
   b. poor results
   c. not special
   d. no difference

7. The Declaration can generally best be summarized as:
   a. We are all equal and should be protected by the law.
   b. We all should prohibit slavery, servitude, torture and punishment.
   c. We are all related and should be treated equally.
   d. We all are to be respected as members of the same family.

8. *Limitation of sovereignty* means ___ .
   a. freedom
   b. equality
   c. restriction
   d. tyranny

Debate

Take one side, add your own ideas and debate in pairs or groups.

For: Everyone should have the same human rights.	*Against:* Human rights are too general and don't suit all countries.
Points:	*Points:*
• Many wars occur because people do not treat others as humans.	• Many rights, such as education, cost money. Not every country can afford them.
• We should treat others as we want to be treated.	• Asian values are different from Western values.
• People of different sexes and backgrounds are equally able.	• Religion is a right, but many religions do not respect other rights.
• _____	• _____
• _____	• _____
• _____	• _____

Debate strategy

When you debate, look for holes, or a lack of facts, in your opponent's argument. Often people will try to sound like they know what they are talking about but don't have any supporting evidence.

Say:
- "While I agree with ... you don't have any facts to support ... ."
- "Your point about ... is correct, but you're very wrong about ... ."

More ideas to debate

"I am not interested in picking up crumbs of compassion thrown from the table of someone who considers himself my master. I want the full menu of rights."
Bishop Desmond Tutu (1931–) South African religious leader and Nobel Peace Prize winner

"Give to every human being every right that you claim for yourself."
Robert Ingersoll (1833–1899) Lawyer

"No man is above the law and no man below it."
Theodore Roosevelt (1858–1919) Former U.S. president

"Whenever I hear anyone arguing for slavery, I feel a strong impulse to see it tried on him personally."
Abraham Lincoln (1809–1865) Former U.S. president

"Silence never won rights. They are not handed down from above; they are forced by pressures from below."
Roger Baldwin (1884–1981) Founder of the American Civil Liberties Union

"I am the inferior of any man whose rights I trample underfoot."
Horace Greeley (1811–1872) Newspaper editor

"I believe in equality for everyone, except reporters and photographers."
Mahatma Gandhi (1869–1948) Indian political leader and reformer

Think about it

Gandhi's life was devoted to the rights of others and this quote is his joke. Why might he have made it?

Learn more

Look for the complete text of the United Nations' Universal Declaration of Human Rights in the library or on the WWW. There are thirty articles in all. Discuss them in class.

Look online

Check out the website at www.read-and-think.com for extra learning resources.

Add new words to your personal dictionary on page 176.

UNIT 3

**Literature
Biography
Culture**

Jane Austen

Lesson One

Before you read

- Who was Jane Austen?
- Why is she famous?

What is happening in the picture?

Couples dance under eighteenth-century chandeliers at this traditional ball

Photo tip

The first photographs
weren't made until
1839. When you
see a photo, you
know it was taken
after then.

- Listen for dates and details about the person's life.

A Romantic Life

Jane Austen

Jane Austen was born on December 16, 1775, in a small village in Hampshire, England, where her father was a minister in the local church. She was the seventh of eight children of the Reverend George Austen and his wife, Cassandra. Jane was mainly educated at home by her parents. In her short life, Jane only ever lived with her family.

Her childhood was very happy. Not only could she play with the other children in her family, but she also got to meet many boys who stayed with the family while her father taught them Greek and Latin. But Jane's lifelong friend and favorite playmate was her older sister, Cassandra, named after her mother. With Cassandra and the other children, Jane often wrote and performed short plays and played charades.

Jane's mother was a lively woman who was fond of reading. As Jane's father was a teacher as well as a minister, the Austen family had an extensive library. Jane loved books, too; she enjoyed reading and also wrote many short satirical stories. Her parents encouraged her, and when she was fourteen, she wrote her first short novel, *Love and Freindship* (sic), with the word friendship misspelled. Later she wrote *A History of England by a partial, prejudiced and ignorant Historian*. It was a humorous view of history and was probably written to make her brothers and sisters laugh.

Language note

The Latin word *sic* means *thus*. It is usually set in parentheses after a misspelling in a quote and shows that the error is the mistake of the first writer or speaker.

Jane became more serious about writing in her early twenties. At this time, there were few opportunities for women of Jane's social class to work. She may have thought that writing a novel might be a way to make some money to help her poor family. She wrote the first drafts of novels that were later to be reworked and published as *Sense and Sensibility*, *Pride and Prejudice* and *Northanger Abbey*. She also began a novel called *The Watsons*, which was never completed.

In many of the novels, there are dances. Jane loved dancing, and was often invited to balls in many of the great houses of the neighborhood. Along with dancing and writing, Jane enjoyed long walks in the countryside with her many friends. Therefore, Jane was truly shocked when her parents told her that they had decided to move to the town of Bath. The reason for the move was mostly to do with Jane and Cassandra: their parents wanted to find husbands for them and thought they were more likely to do so in a busy town such as Bath.

But the next four years the family spent in Bath were miserable for Jane, who felt she did not fit in and missed her country life. This changed in 1805, when Jane's father died. Jane, Cassandra and their mother had to move and were suddenly poor. Fortunately, her brothers helped. During this time, Jane fell in love, but the young man died soon after they met. Jane accepted an offer of marriage from a wealthy landowner, who was a brother of some of her closest friends, but she changed her mind the next morning. Jane Austen, a young woman who wrote so much about love and marriage, never married.

Chawton House, where Jane Austen revised her novels

One of her brothers, Edward, had been very fortunate. An uncle had adopted Edward and left him his fortune. In 1809, Edward gave Jane, Cassandra and their mother a small but comfortable house in the countryside with a pretty garden.

Computer note

When you read about something new, it can help to use the computer to find pictures to help you understand. For example, you can search Jane Austen on the WWW and see the places she lived.

In a comfortable chair at a small round table Jane revised *Sense and Sensibility* (1811), *Pride and Prejudice* (1813), *Mansfield Park* (1814), *Emma* (1816) and *Persuasion*. *Persuasion* was published together with *Northanger Abbey* in 1818, the year after she died. Since then, all the books have been reprinted and read continuously and all have been made into popular movies. 60

(621 words)

Vocabulary notes

1. **ball** (noun) a large formal occasion at which people dance
2. **charades** (noun) a game in which one person uses actions and no words to show the meaning of a word or phrase, and other people have to guess what it is
3. **draft** (noun) a piece of writing or a plan that is not yet in its finished form
4. **landowner** (noun) someone who owns land, especially a large amount of it
5. **minister** (noun) a priest in some Christian churches
6. **miserable** (adjective) extremely unhappy, for example because you feel lonely, cold, or badly treated
7. **revise** (verb) to change something because of new information or ideas
8. **satirical** (adjective) a way of criticizing something such as a group of people or a system, in which you deliberately make them seem funny so that people will see their faults

Add new words to your personal dictionary on page 176.

Read and listen again to practice your pronunciation.

A. Answer these questions.

1. Why might Jane Austen not have gone to school?
2. Why did the Austen family move to Bath?
3. Where did Jane finish most of her novels?
4. Who was Jane's best friend?
5. How old was Jane when she died?

Understand what you read

Biography

A biography tells the story of a person's life. Usually, biographies start with when the person was born and ends with his or her death. Biographies include significant dates and events as well as anecdotes—small stories—that help illustrate something about a person's character.

Not everything in a person's life is included in a biography. Much of what someone does day-to-day or even for several years might be quite boring. In other cases, someone might have done one amazing, unexpected thing that takes up most of the biography.

Here are four tips for reading biographies:

a. Concentrate on the dates, considering how old the person was at each stage.
b. Think about why the biographer (the writer of the biography) has included each anecdote and each part of the person's life.
c. Good biographies give contrasts between how someone started and what they achieved.
d. An autobiography is a biography written by someone to tell his or her own life story.

B. Match these examples to the tips.

1. _____ I decided to tell the story of my life to let the world know what it is like to be a lion tamer.
2. _____ Although she was born penniless, she became one of the wealthiest people in the world.

3. _____ They first found she was musical when she was five and she sat at the piano and played a complete sonata.

4. _____ He was born in 1915, but by the time World War II began in 1939, he was already a general in the army.

C. Read and answer the questions.

1. How long did Jane have to wait for *Pride and Prejudice* to be published?
2. How did the novel change from when Jane first wrote it?

Since it was first published in 1813, *Pride and Prejudice* has always been Jane Austen's most popular novel. It portrays the initial misunderstandings and later growing love between the witty Elizabeth Bennet and the aristocratic Fitzwilliam Darcy. The title *Pride and Prejudice* refers to the ways in which Elizabeth and Darcy first think about each other. The original version of the novel was written around 1796 with the title *First Impressions*. It was probably written as a series of letters rather than a story. In 1797, Jane Austen's father tried to sell it to a publisher who turned it down without even reading it.

D. Fill in the missing words. Use the correct form of the word.

- **caprice** (noun) a sudden and unreasonable change of mind or behavior
- **character** (noun) the particular combination of qualities that makes someone a particular type of person
- **excitable** (adjective) becoming excited too easily
- **nerves** (noun) used to talk about someone being worried or frightened
- **sarcastic** (adjective) saying things that are the opposite of what you mean, in order to make an unkind joke or to show that you are annoyed

Mr. Bennet was an odd mixture of _____ humour, seriousness, and _____ . He had been married twenty-three years but his wife still did not understand his _____ . Mrs. Bennet's mind was less difficult to understand. She was _____ , knew little and was frequently angry. When she was unhappy, she blamed her _____ . The business of her life was to get her daughters married.

What does the last sentence tell you about Mrs. Bennet's character?

What about you?

Could you write a Jane Austen novel? Perhaps. Match words and phrases from each column to describe five interesting characters at the start of a story.

An old	man	steals	a fortune	then suddenly ...
A young	woman	owns	a lost map	then fortunately ...
A poor	child	finds	a grave	then sadly ...
A rich	stranger	loses	a love letter	then quickly ...
A foolish	criminal	makes	a large house	then slowly ...
A wise	heir	notices	a horse	then never ...

Lesson Two

Read about it

- What is the tone of the chapter?
- How does Mr. Bennet tease Mrs. Bennet?

Pride and Prejudice

by Jane Austen

Excerpt from the first chapter

It is a truth universally acknowledged, that a single man in possession of a good fortune must be in want of a wife.

5 However little known the feelings or views of such a man may be on his first entering a neighbourhood, this truth is so well fixed in the minds of the surrounding families, that he is 10 considered as the rightful property of some one or other of their daughters.

"My dear Mr. Bennet," said his lady to him one day, "have you heard that Netherfield Park is let at last?"

Mr. Bennet replied that he had not. 15

"But it is," returned she; "for Mrs. Long has just been here, and she told me all about it."

Mr. Bennet made no answer.

Reading strategy

When reading a novel, learn the names of all the characters as soon as possible and keep pictures of them in your mind. It makes it easier to follow the story.

Concepts

Older books often use language in a different way and include terms that are difficult to understand. When Mr. Bennet refers to *his lady*, it's easy to guess it's his wife and also understand that an *establishment* is a large house. But it's more difficult to know that a *chaise and four* refers to a carriage drawn by four horses and that *Netherfield Park* refers not to a public park but to a grand house and its grounds.

20 "Do not you want to know who has taken it?" cried his wife impatiently.

"You want to tell me, and I have no objection to hearing it."

This was invitation enough.

25 "Why, my dear, you must know, Mrs. Long says that Netherfield is taken by a young man of large fortune from the north of England; that he came down on Monday in a chaise and four to see 30 the place, and was so much delighted with it that he agreed with Mr. Morris immediately; that he is to take possession before Michaelmas, and some of his servants are to be in the 35 house by the end of next week."

"What is his name?"

"Bingley."

"Is he married or single?"

"Oh! single, my dear, to be sure! A 40 single man of large fortune; four or five thousand a year. What a fine thing for our girls!"

"How so? How can it affect them?"

"My dear Mr. Bennet," replied his 45 wife, "how can you be so tiresome!

You must know that I am thinking of his marrying one of them."

"Is that his design in settling here?"

"Design! nonsense, how can you talk so! But it is very likely that he may 50 fall in love with one of them, and therefore you must visit him as soon as he comes."

"I see no occasion for that. You and the girls may go, or you may send 55 them by themselves, which perhaps will be still better; for, as you are as handsome as any of them, Mr. Bingley might like you the best of the party."

"My dear, you flatter me. I certainly 60 have had my share of beauty, but I do not pretend to be anything extraordinary now. When a woman has five grown up daughters, she ought to give over thinking of her own 65 beauty."

"In such cases, a woman has not often much beauty to think of."

"But, my dear, you must indeed go and see Mr. Bingley when he comes 70 into the neighbourhood."

"It is more than I engage for, I assure you."

"But consider your daughters. Only think what an establishment it would be for one of them. Sir William and Lady Lucas are determined to go, merely on that account, for in general, you know they visit no newcomers. Indeed you must go, for it will be impossible for us to visit him, if you do not."

"You are over-scrupulous, surely. I dare say Mr. Bingley will be very glad to see you; and I will send a few lines by you to assure him of my hearty consent to his marrying which ever he chooses of the girls; though I must throw in a good word for my little Lizzy."

"I desire you will do no such thing. Lizzy is not a bit better than the others; and I am sure she is not half so handsome as Jane, nor half so good humoured as Lydia. But you are always giving her the preference."

"They have none of them much to recommend them," replied he; "they are all silly and ignorant like other girls; but Lizzy has something more of quickness than her sisters."

(652 words)

Vocabulary notes

1. **flatter** (verb) to praise someone in order to please them or get something from them, even though you do not mean it
2. **Michaelmas** (noun) September 29, a Christian holy day in honor of Saint Michael
3. **possession** (noun) if something is in your possession, you own it, or you have obtained it from somewhere
4. **preference** (noun) if you have a preference for something, you like it more than another thing and will choose it if you can
5. **scrupulous** (adjective) very careful to be completely honest and fair

 Read and listen again to practice your pronunciation.

After you read

A. Summarize the main idea in one sentence.

In the middle of *Pride and Prejudice*, Darcy finds himself falling in love not only with Elizabeth's beauty, but also with her intelligence and wit. He also likes the fact that she is not intimidated by him, even though he is rich and powerful. He proposes marriage, but makes a mess of it, bringing up all her faults and those of her family. She is angry and refuses him, then criticizes him in turn.

B. Vocabulary check: Fill in the missing letters to find the secret word.

```
        p  o  s [S] e  s  s  i  o  n
              f  l [ ] t  t  e  r
     s  a  r  c  a  s [ ] i  c
           e  x  c [ ] t  a  b  l  e
           c  a  p [ ] i  c  e
                 m [ ] n  i  s  t  e  r
                    [ ] h  a  r  a  d  e  s
              c  h [ ] r  a  c  t  e  r
     s  c  r  u  p  u [ ] o  u  s
```

Language note

An *adaptation* is a story, play or movie made from an earlier work. These sometimes change the context such as in *Clueless*, a movie based on Jane Austen's novel *Emma*, but set today in Beverley Hills with rich spoiled teenagers.

C. Choose the best answer.

1. A synonym for *design* in the second passage is ___ .
   a. illustration
   b. architectural drawing
   c. reason
   d. printed pattern

2. An example of a satirical title of Jane Austen's writing is ___ .
   a. *Mansfield Park*
   b. *Pride and Prejudice*
   c. *Love and Freindship*
   d. *A History of England by a partial, prejudiced and ignorant Historian*

3. Why was Jane Austen shocked at the move to Bath?
   a. She thought she might make money for her family.
   b. She loved dancing and was invited to balls.
   c. She loved the countryside.
   d. She didn't want to get married.

4. An irony of Jane Austen's life was that ___ .
   a. *Northanger Abbey* was published a year after she died
   b. Jane wrote of love and marriage, but never married
   c. Jane loved the country, but lived in the city
   d. Jane fell in love, but the young man died soon after

5. The family suddenly became poor because Jane's ___ .
   a. family moved to Bath
   b. father died
   c. books were not popular
   d. refusal to marry annoyed her family

6. The first sentence of the second passage means that ___ .
   a. everyone knows that rich men must marry
   b. it is known that single men possess money and want wives
   c. throughout the world, men are lucky to have wives
   d. it is the truth that all rich young men are in search of wives

7. *A young man of large fortune* is ___ .
   a. a man who has experienced good and bad things in life
   b. a man with good luck
   c. a rich man
   d. a man in a good situation

8. *Netherfield Park is let at last* means it was ___ .
   a. wished
   b. suggested
   c. allowed
   d. rented

Exam strategy

The order you choose to answer the questions doesn't matter; first answer the questions that are easiest for you. But mark the questions you haven't answered so you don't forget to go back to them.

Debate

Take one side, add your own ideas and debate in pairs or groups.

For: Everyone wants the same things in life.

Points:

• Most people follow the same path, growing up, getting married and having children.

• Jane Austen's novels are popular because they show people's basic desires.

• Many of the characters in Jane Austen's novels are easily recognized all around us.

• _____

• _____

• _____

Against: People are individuals, with individual desires.

Points:

• For a long time, economic pressures forced people to take the same paths, but that is changing.

• Life is not like novels, all with happy endings.

• Much has changed in the world since Jane Austen was born.

• _____

• _____

• _____

Debate strategy

When you debate, quote your opponent to show that you understand what they are talking about. Then give your point of view.

Say:

• "You say that you believe ... but in fact ... ."
• "What you're trying to say is ... but the truth is ... ."

More ideas to debate

Quotes from Jane Austen and her work
"Nobody ever acts, suffers or enjoys, as one expects."
Letter to her sister Cassandra, June 30, 1808

"If there is any thing disagreeable going on, men are always sure to get out of it."
Persuasion

"I wish as well as everybody else to be perfectly happy; but like everybody else it must be in my own way."
Sense and Sensibility

"If I loved you less, I might be able to talk about it more."
Emma

"... do anything other than marry without affection."
Pride and Prejudice

"There are secrets in all families, you know ... ."
Emma

"For what do we live, but to make sport for our neighbours, and laugh at them in our turn?"
Pride and Prejudice

Learn more

Summaries and full versions of all of Jane Austen's novels are available in libraries and on the WWW. Find examples and report them to your class.

Look online

Check out the website at www.read-and-think.com for extra learning resources.

Add new words to your personal dictionary on page 176.

Do You Believe in Ghosts?

Lesson One

Before you read

- Do you believe in ghosts?
- What different kinds of ghosts are there?

What is happening in the picture?

Ghosts—and ghost stories—are timeless phenomena

Read about it

- Listen for ways people try to contact ghosts.

Looking for Ghosts!

Among all the things in the world that frighten people, ghosts are among the scariest.

At Halloween, children dress up as ghosts and other supernatural creatures to scare their friends. Ghosts, like many of these other creatures, have a long history. Ancient tales of cultures all around the world are full of ghost stories. 5 Often these ghosts are the spirits of the dead who come back to Earth for some reason.

Harry Houdini near a model of Abraham Lincoln, as he attempts to talk to the deceased U.S. president

What that reason is, supposedly differs from ghost to ghost. Some ghosts are reluctant to leave their 10 favorite place. They have lived in the same house, for example, for all their lives and even death cannot convince them to completely leave. Others are said to come back to avenge their own 15 murders. If a person has had his or her life cut short, their ghost might want to make sure that someone is punished for the crime. Many ghosts are supposedly from those who were wrongly executed. 20

But are there such things as ghosts? Many people think so, but how do you prove whether or not ghosts really exist?

Many people have tried over the years, but sometimes the ways of looking for ghosts have been just a way to cheat people. The most common way is using some kind of tool to contact the spirit world. For example, a board on which one or more people put their fingers and are directed to a yes/no answer or individual letters that spell out a message.

Scientists claim that this type of message is just a trick of our brains, which have deep thoughts about what we want the board to say. Of course we get the answer we want.

Others are more direct, with people who claim to speak to ghosts and write down their thoughts. These people are said to channel the ideas of the dead, and some, with no talent in music or writing, have been seen to write music, poems or novels in the style of long-dead famous people.

Scientists looking at these are often unimpressed with the results and suggest that the new writing may just be the brain reworking familiar styles.

In other cases, ghosts are said to speak to spiritualists in séances, where several people gather, usually in a dark room, to hear messages from dead relatives and friends. Sometimes it is for love; sometimes it is for something else. For example, someone might die without telling a relative where they have hidden all their money!

In such séances, there are sometimes more dramatic events. For example, a ghost appears or the cold hand of a dead child seems to touch the arm of its sad mother. More often, it is a parent that is sought.

Someone who desperately wanted to talk to his mother after her death in 1920 was Harry Houdini (1874–1926). Houdini was best known for his magic tricks on stage, such as his escapes from being tied up with rope or locked in chains. As a magician, he knew the tricks other people used so, after being disappointed time and again in the search for his mother, he started on a new career. In this career, Houdini went to séances—often in disguise with a journalist and a policeman— and watched and listened closely to find out how things were being done. He also helped *Scientific American* magazine, which offered a huge cash prize to anyone who could prove ghosts existed, but no one could fool Harry Houdini!

Concepts

Spiritualism is the belief that some people can talk to the *spirits* or *ghosts* of the dead. People who do this are often called *spiritualists* or *mediums* and summon ghosts at meetings called *séances*.

Houdini shows in a séance how mediums can ring bells using their toes

But how does this explain why some places appear to be haunted, sometimes reported by strangers over hundreds of years? How is it that these strangers allege to have seen a special ghost without any prior knowledge? |55 |60

Recently, psychologists in the United Kingdom had volunteers visit so-called haunted mansions and vaults in England and Scotland. While they found no evidence for ghosts, paradoxically, the psychologists explained that some people do often report feeling ghosts present in certain places. Their explanation is that a cluster of features, such as changes in light and temperature, make certain people "feel" that a ghost is there. |65

What would Harry Houdini say? |70

(689 words)

Vocabulary notes

1. **allege** (verb) to say that something is true or that someone has done something wrong, although it has not been proved
2. **cluster** (noun) a group of things of the same kind that are very close together
3. **execute** (verb) to kill someone, especially legally as a punishment
4. **haunt** (verb) if the soul of a dead person haunts a place, it appears there often
5. **paradoxically** (adverb) in a way that is surprising because it is the opposite of what you would expect
6. **prior** (adjective) existing or arranged before something else or before the present situation
7. **volunteer** (noun) someone who is willing to offer help

Add new words to your personal dictionary on page 176.

Read and listen again to practice your pronunciation.

A. Answer these questions.

1. For what reasons might ghosts come back to Earth?
2. What is a séance?
3. Who was Harry Houdini and what was his first occupation?
4. Why was Houdini interested in ghosts?
5. What can make people seem to "feel" ghosts?

Understand what you read

Reported speech

Reported speech, also called indirect speech, refers to one or more sentences reporting what someone has said. It is used in both spoken and written English.

If the reporting verb, such as *say* or *ask*, is in the past tense, e.g., *said*, the reported clause is also in a past form.

- *"I like ghosts," he said.* becomes *He said he liked ghosts.*

If the reporting verb is in the present, present perfect or the future tense, the tense form in the reported speech can be left unchanged.

- *"I like meeting ghosts," she says.* becomes *She says she likes meeting ghosts.*

If reporting a general truth, the present tense will be retained.

- *The teacher said phrasal verbs are very important.*

Here are four tips for working with reported speech:

- Pronouns change to match the subject of the sentence, e.g., *I* becomes *he* or *she*; *we* becomes *they*, *my* becomes *his* or *her*.
- Adverbs of time change to match the time of speaking, e.g., *tomorrow* becomes *the next day*; *yesterday* becomes *the day before*.
- Yes/no questions use *if*: *"Do you want to see a ghost?"* becomes *She asked me if I wanted to see a ghost.*
- General truths in the present tense are reported in the present tense, e.g., *She said ghosts are common all around the world.*

Language note

When you are reading reported speech, you often find that it is a summary of what the person has said, without quotation marks, rather than every word that was spoken.

B. Read these sentences and change to reported speech.

1. "The ghost led us to the treasure," they said.

   _____

2. "I love old castles," she says.

   _____

3. "Do you often see spirits with knives?" Mary asked.

   _____

4. "We hope to see a phantom tonight," they said.

   _____

5. "A poltergeist came into my room last night," he said.

   _____

C. Number these sentences in order.

_____I woke in the middle of the night with a sudden chill.

_____It was a dark and moonless night; I followed her across the roof.

__1__It was my first night in the ancient castle.

_____She looked back, smiled and disappeared.

_____She smiled and gestured for me to follow her through a secret door onto the castle roof.

_____Suddenly, I stopped. I looked closely and saw that she had stepped off the roof and I was just about to fall.

_____The ghost of a young girl was standing near my bed.

__8__The next morning, I heard that 100 years ago a young girl had been chased across the roof and fell to her death.

D. Fill in the missing words. Use the correct form of the word.

- **custom** (noun) something that is done by people in a particular society because it is traditional
- **ghost story** (noun) a story about ghosts that is intended to frighten people
- **journalist** (noun) someone who writes news reports for newspapers, magazines, television or radio
- **samurai** (noun) a member of a powerful military class in Japan in the past
- **supernatural** (noun) events, powers, and creatures that cannot be explained, and seem to involve gods or magic

Lafcadio Hearn (1850–1904) did more than anyone else before him to introduce Japan's _____ to English readers. He was born in Lefkas, Greece, son of an Irish doctor and his Greek wife. As a _____ in the United States, he was sent to Japan, but quit when he arrived and became an English teacher. He married the daughter of a _____ . He became a Japanese citizen and wrote a great deal about Japan and the _____ . After reading a _____, he decided to collect several and published them in books.

What ghost stories do you know?

What about you?

What would you do if you saw a ghost? Would you be frightened? What questions would you want to ask a ghost?

Lesson Two

Read about it

- What is a ghost story?
- How does the author keep your attention?

A Dead Secret

Adapted from a story by Lafcadio Hearn

Lafcadio Hearn, ca. 1890s

A long time ago, there lived a rich merchant who had a daughter called O-Sono. As she was very clever and pretty, he thought it would be a pity to let her grow up only having been taught by country teachers. So he sent her to Kyoto, to be trained by the ladies of the capital. After, she was married to a merchant friend of her father's family and lived happily with him for nearly four years. They had one child, but then O-Sono fell ill and died.

On the night after her funeral, her little son said that his mamma had come back and was in the room upstairs. She had smiled at him, but would not talk to him, so he became afraid and ran away. Some of the family went upstairs to O-Sono's room and were startled to see the figure of the dead mother. She appeared in front of a *tansu*, or chest of drawers, that still

49

contained her clothes and ornaments. Her head and shoulders could be very distinctly seen; but from the waist downward the figure thinned into invisibility.

Then the folk were afraid and left the room. Below they consulted. One said, "A woman is fond of her small things; and O-Sono was much attached to her belongings. Perhaps she has come back to look at them. Many dead persons will do that, unless the things are given to the local temple. If we do this, her spirit will probably find rest."

It was agreed that this be done as soon as possible. So the following morning the drawers were emptied and all of O-Sono's ornaments and clothing were taken to the temple. But she came back the next night and looked at the *tansu* as before. And she came back every night. The house became a house of fear.

O-Sono's husband went to the temple priest for advice. The priest said, "There must be something about which she is anxious, in or near that *tansu*."

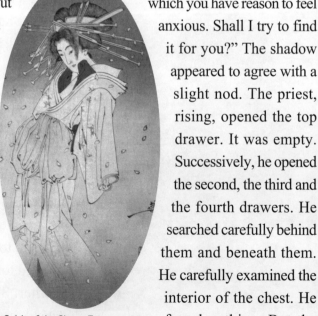

The Spirit of the Cherry Tree, ca. 1890s

"But we emptied all the drawers," replied the husband. "There is nothing in the *tansu*."

"Well, tonight I shall go to your house, and keep watch in that room and see what can be done. No one can enter the room while I am watching, unless I call."

After sundown, the priest went to the house and entered the room. For a long time, nothing happened. Then the figure of O-Sono suddenly appeared in front of the *tansu*. She kept her eyes fixed upon the *tansu*.

The priest said, "I have come here in order to help you. Perhaps in that *tansu* there is something about which you have reason to feel anxious. Shall I try to find it for you?" The shadow appeared to agree with a slight nod. The priest, rising, opened the top drawer. It was empty. Successively, he opened the second, the third and the fourth drawers. He searched carefully behind them and beneath them. He carefully examined the interior of the chest. He found nothing. But the figure remained gazing as before. "What can she want?" thought the priest. Suddenly, it occurred to him that there might be something hidden under the paper that lined the drawers. He removed the lining of the first drawer—nothing! He removed the lining of the second and third drawers—still nothing. But under the lining of the fourth drawer he found a letter.

"Is this what has troubled you?" he asked. The shadow of the woman turned toward him and gazed at the letter. "Shall I burn it for you?" he asked. She bowed before him. "It shall be burned in the temple this very morning," he promised. "And no one shall read it, except me." The figure smiled and vanished.

Dawn was breaking as the priest went downstairs. The family waited anxiously below. "Do not worry," he said. "She will not appear again." And she never did.

The letter was burned. It was a love letter written to O-Sono at the time of her studies in Kyoto. But the priest alone knew what was in it; and the secret died with him.

(687 words)

Reading strategy

Different kinds of writing use different techniques to get readers' attention. Ghost stories use mystery and suspense to build attention, usually leading to a surprise ending.

Vocabulary notes

1. **anxious** (adjective) worried about something
2. **be attached to sb/sth** (verb) to like someone or something very much, because you have known them or had them for a long time
3. **consult** (verb) to ask for information or advice from someone because it is their job to know something
4. **invisibility** (noun) something that is invisible cannot be seen
5. **lining** (noun) a piece of material that covers the inside of something, especially a piece of clothing
6. **merchant** (noun) someone whose job is to buy and sell wine, coal, etc., or a small company that does this
7. **ornament** (noun) a small object that you keep in your house because it is beautiful rather than useful

Read and listen again to practice your pronunciation.

After you read

A. Summarize the main idea in one sentence.

One theory about ghosts is that they are people who are troubled by something left undone on Earth. They return to "haunt" a place because, for example, their killer has not been punished or something special has not been shared. Many stories feature ghosts who lead fearful relatives to hidden treasures.

B. Vocabulary check: Fill in the missing letters to find the secret word.

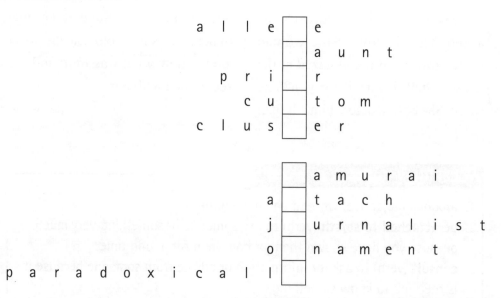

a l l e ☐ e

☐ a u n t

p r i ☐ r

c u ☐ t o m

c l u s ☐ e r

☐ a m u r a i

a ☐ t a c h

j ☐ u r n a l i s t

o ☐ n a m e n t

p a r a d o x i c a l l ☐

C. Choose the best answer.

1. Ghosts may return to Earth if they were ___ .
   a. unhappy in heaven
   b. still alive
   c. executed for a good reason
   d. murdered or unjustly executed

2. A séance is a kind of ___ .
   a. tea
   b. ghost
   c. spiritualist
   d. meeting

3. People who write ghost stories and music ___ .
   a. would be more impressive if their work was good
   b. must use a feather pen
   c. don't like to talk with ghosts
   d. don't necessarily believe in ghosts

4. The fact that Houdini brought a policeman to the séances suggests ___ .
   a. policemen enjoy meeting ghosts
   b. policemen often arrest ghosts
   c. spiritualists sometimes cheat
   d. Houdini was afraid of ghosts

5. Houdini helped *Scientific American* ___ .
   a. write stories about ghosts
   b. sell magazines
   c. prove ghosts exist
   d. find out how ghost tricks were done

6. The reader can infer that the letter in the second passage was written by ___ .
   a. her former lover
   b. her loving husband
   c. her dead father
   d. her caring son

7. *Thinned into invisibility* means ___ .
   a. liquified
   b. left
   c. disappeared
   d. was very slender

8. A synonym for *anxious* is ___ .
   a. feeling worried
   b. touch strongly
   c. wanting something
   d. seems strange

9. "I have come here in order to help you," the priest said, could be reported as:
   a. He said I have come here in order to help you.
   b. He said he had come there in order to help you.
   c. He said I had come here in order to help her.
   d. He said he had come there in order to help her.

10. A *slight nod* is ___ .
    a. a happy look
    b. a hand gesture
    c. a head movement
    d. a step forward

Exam strategy

In writing exams, take time to reread the question as you write to make sure you have not gone off the topic.

53

Debate

Take one side, add your own ideas and debate in pairs or groups.

For: Ghosts must exist.

Points:

- Ghost stories are common to cultures all over the world.

- Some ghosts have been seen for hundreds of years by different people.

- There are too many unexplained events around ghost stories.

- _____

- _____

- _____

Against: Ghosts do not exist.

Points:

- There is not a good photographic record of a ghost.

- Ghost stories just reflect people's fear of death.

- Ghosts are just something to frighten children.

- _____

- _____

- _____

Debate strategy

When you debate, don't be fooled by sweeping general statements. Ask for more information when your opponent uses phrases such as, *hundreds of years* or *many countries.*

Say:

- "Excuse me, could you be more specific? Exactly how long was it?"
- "Excuse me, but that's too general. Please give an example."

Another idea to debate

Some ghosts may be nothing more than the human mind feeling guilty. Someone might "see" the ghost of a relative because they feel guilty that they did not treat that relative well during his or her lifetime. Similarly, when we are alone in the dark, we might see a ghost because we are afraid of the dark and a "ghost" gives us a better reason to feel as we do.

Learn more

There are countless ghost stories. Many, such as Oscar Wilde's *The Canterville Ghost* and others collected by Lafcadio Hearn, are available in the library or on the WWW. Find a short ghost story and report it to your class.

Look online

Check out the website at www.read-and-think.com for extra learning resources.

Add new words to your personal dictionary on page 176.

You Are What You Eat!

Lesson One

Before you read

- Where does chocolate come from?
- How did chocolate change after Europeans started using it?

What is happening in the picture?

Peasant Wedding Feast, by Pieter Bruegel the Elder, 1568

Reading strategy

Captions do not always repeat what is in a picture. Instead, they add information or help you to interpret what the picture is showing.

- Listen for events that changed the idea of chocolate.

A Short History of Chocolate

Chocolate was unknown in Europe until after 1492, when Christopher Columbus (1451–1506) returned from the first European explorations in the New World. What would eventually become the favorite food and drink of millions took a long time and many innovations to become popular.

Cacao pods

Columbus, who thought he had reached India, not a new continent, returned with many new treasures, many of them agricultural. He presented them all to his patrons, the Spanish King Ferdinand (1452–1516) and his wife, Queen Isabella (1451–1504). They were probably not impressed with their first view of the small dark bitter cocoa beans, and could not have imagined how these beans might one day become the source of an international chocolate industry.

The first person to turn cocoa beans into something commercially important was the Spanish explorer Hernando Cortez (1485–1547). Cortez is most remembered for his brutal conquest of Mexico. When introduced to the Aztec Emperor Montezuma in 1519, he and his men were offered grand gold cups of the emperor's royal drink, *chocolatl,* meaning warm liquid. Montezuma

5

10

15

20

evidently drank fifty or more cups of it daily.

However, the Spanish soldiers were more impressed by the gold cups than the drink. The Aztec preparation of *chocolatl* did nothing to change the cocoa bean's natural bitterness. To adjust the drink for European tastes, Cortez and others decided to sweeten it with cane sugar.

When they took this sweetened *chocolatl* back to Spain, the drink became popular, especially when combined with several other newly-discovered spices, such as cinnamon, vanilla and even hot chili pepper. Eventually, people began to serve *chocolatl* as a hot drink.

Statue of Christopher Columbus

Hot chocolate soon became all the rage among the Spanish aristocracy and Spain established cocoa plantations in its new colonies. But the Spanish carefully guarded the secrets of *chocolatl* production, and more than a hundred years would pass before the process was revealed by monks, whose job it was to work with the raw ingredients.

Making chocolate

Chocolatl spread throughout Europe and was made fashionable by various kings and queens. The habit of chocolate drinking spread to England, where in 1657, the first of many famous chocolate houses appeared.

Eventually, the traditional methods of making chocolate by hand, used by small shops, gave way to mass production and the use of steam engines to help in the cocoa grinding process. By 1730, chocolate had dropped in price so most people could afford to drink it. The invention of the cocoa press in 1828 reduced the price even further and helped to improve the quality of the beverage by 55 squeezing out part of the cocoa butter, the fat that occurs naturally in cocoa beans. Chocolate tasted much more like what we are now used to.

In the nineteenth century, two major improvements were made to chocolate. The first came in 1847, when an English company introduced a smooth chocolate for eating. The second development occurred in 1876, in Vevey, 60 Switzerland, when Daniel Peter found a way to add milk to chocolate, creating the product we enjoy today known as milk chocolate.

(507 words)

Reading strategy

Dates of centuries can be confusing. The *1500s* were from 1500 to 1599. The *fifteenth century* was from 1400 to 1499.

Vocabulary notes

1. **all the rage** (phrase) to be very popular or fashionable
2. **aristocracy** (noun) the people in the highest social class, who traditionally have a lot of land, money, and power
3. **habit** (noun) something that you do regularly or usually, often without thinking about it because you have done it so many times before
4. **monk** (noun) a member of an all-male religious group that lives apart from other people in a monastery

Add new words to your personal dictionary on page 176.

Read and listen again to practice your pronunciation.

After you read

A. Answer these questions.

1. What was chocolate originally called?
2. What did the word mean?
3. What extra ingredient made chocolate more popular?
4. How did Daniel Peter improve chocolate?
5. When was solid chocolate for eating introduced?

Understand what you read

Idioms

Idioms are expressions that are used to describe something, often humorously. Sometimes they are used simply as a shorter explanation. For example, a *coffee break* does not mean you have to drink coffee when you pause from your work; you may do many other things in the same time. If you don't already know the idiom, it can be difficult to understand what it means. Sometimes, you can guess from the context or simply by using common sense. For example, a *half-baked idea*, is easy to understand as an unfinished idea.

Here are four tips for working with idioms:
- Idioms are most often used in informal speech and writing.
- Many idioms can be understood by the context.
- Idioms often show the writer's attitude toward the topic.
- Looking up individual words in an idiom seldom helps you understand it; none of the food idioms below describe anything to do with food.

Reading strategy

Increase your comprehension by looking for related idioms. For example, *salt* is used in many idioms about money because ancient Roman soldiers were once paid in salt.

B. Draw lines between these food idioms and their definitions.

1. eat dirt
2. spill the beans
3. piece of cake
4. egg on
5. cut the mustard
6. salt of the earth

a. an easy task
b. succeed
c. accept an insult
d. tell a secret
e. ordinary but honest person
f. urge someone on

C. Summarize the reading by writing short notes next to each year.

1492: _____

1519: _____

1657: _____

1730: _____

1847: _____

1876: _____

D. Fill in the missing words. Use the correct form of the word.

- **adore** (verb) to like something very much
- **customer** (noun) someone who buys goods or services from a shop, company, etc.
- **introduce** (verb) to bring a type of thing somewhere for the first time
- **reject** (verb) to refuse to accept, believe in, or agree with something
- **ridiculous** (adjective) very silly or unreasonable

French fries, potatoes cut into strips and fried in oil, became popular in the 1700s in France and the dish was _____ to the United States by Thomas Jefferson (1743–1826), later a president of the U.S. In 1853, George Crum was working as chef in a restaurant near New York when a _____ sent back his order of French fries, saying they were too thick. Crum tried again, but the second order was also _____. Crum decided to make some _____ French fries and sliced them so thin that they would break if you tried to eat them with a fork. The customer and everyone else _____ them and the potato chip was born.

Reading strategy

To make a passage more interesting, writers use different words or phrases. In this paragraph, *U.S.* is used instead of repeating *United States*.

What other fast foods do you like? What are the stories behind them?

What about you?

What did you eat yesterday? Look on the WWW and try to find what someone in another country eats in one day as typical meals. You might be surprised.

Lesson Two

- What is a calorie?
- How are weight and exercise related?

How Much Do You Eat? How Much Do You Burn?

For most of history, people's biggest problem has been getting enough to eat. Five hundred years ago, all but the richest people would have had great difficulty hunting, gathering or farming their own food. Some were luckier than others, such as people who lived near oceans full of seafood. But elsewhere getting fed was a struggle, especially during winter. Today, in the developed world, the opposite is true. Too many people eat too much. Or rather, they do not balance what they eat with how much energy they use.

One of the clearest examples of this is the emergence of fat "little emperors" in China. With the one-child policy, fewer children are being born but still have the affection of parents and grandparents who translate love into giving children more food than they need. In turn, these children become greedy and want to eat excessive amounts of junk food, foods that are full of fat but offer little energy.

You need to eat because food gives you energy. This energy is usually measured in calories. Technically, a calorie is the amount of heat required to raise the

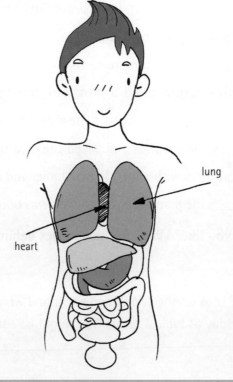

lung

heart

temperature of a gram of water one degree Celsius. Part of your body's need for energy is just to support your basic life systems. But you also need food for the extra energy required whenever you undertake any physical activity—even just moving your eyes to read this page!

When you rest, watch TV or sleep, your body is still working. This is because your lungs need energy to filter oxygen from the air you breathe. Also, your heart needs energy to pump the oxygen-enriched blood to your body's cells and organs. Your body is always repairing, replacing and cleaning parts of itself. It has to control its temperature, even when you are sleeping. When you are awake, your body needs even more energy because your heart beats faster and your lungs work harder.

The energy you need comes from two places: the food that you eat and the energy stored as fat in your body. Fat is distributed all over your body, but excess fat is mostly found on the hips and thighs of women and around the abdomens of men. We all eat different amounts, depending on both our sizes and how active we are. Generally, an adult man eats about 2,500 calories of food a day. To be healthy, this should include about 83 grams of fat, 60 grams of protein and 25 grams of fiber, as well as various minerals and vitamins.

When you want to put on weight, the solution is easy. Eat more, consuming more calories. When you want to lose weight, you generally have to eat less, consuming fewer calories, but you also have to exercise. The reason exercise is important has to do with how your body works. Actually, your body doesn't like to lose weight. So when you eat less, it does not automatically start using up fat. Usually, you will lose liquids instead, and then even muscle. People who go without food for a long time often weaken the muscles of their hearts and lose minerals such as potassium, and this is what kills them.

When you exercise, you have a choice of many different activities and they don't need to be too strenuous, but they should be regular and take up twenty to thirty minutes each day. To keep your heart healthy, vigorous exercise three times a week is also recommended.

This chart shows how many calories you burn in twenty to thirty minutes, doing a few common activities.

Activity	Intensity	Calories Used
Volleyball	Moderate	70
Walking, moderate pace	Moderate	81
Walking, brisk pace	Moderate	94
Table tennis	Moderate	94
Social dancing	Moderate	103
Jogging	Hard	167
Running	Very Hard	231

A hamburger is usually somewhere between 250 and 600 calories. How long would it take you to burn it off?

Source: Adapted from the Surgeon General's Report on Physical Activity and Health, 1996

⁹⁵ But what about people who don't like to exercise? What do they do? Many engage in strange diets. Generally, these are not helpful.

Weight may disappear for a short time, but it almost always returns.

(697 words)

Vocabulary notes

1. **emergence** (noun) when something begins to be known or noticed
2. **excessive** (adjective) much more than is reasonable or necessary
3. **strenuous** (adjective) needing a lot of effort or strength
4. **technically** (adverb) according to the exact details of a rule or law
5. **translate** (verb) to change something, or be changed, from one form into another
6. **vigorous** (adjective) using a lot of energy and strength or determination

Listen

Read and listen again to practice your pronunciation.

Discussion

After you read

A. Summarize the main idea in one sentence.

Have you looked at the cover of a fashion magazine lately? The women featured, so-called supermodels, tend to look the same: tall and thin to the point of starvation. The fashion industry that supports such magazines is often blamed for poor health and deaths among teenage girls. The reason is that some young girls see these women as role models and try desperately to look the same. Instead, these girls should be happy with their own looks and spend time improving themselves in ways other than foolish diets.

_____

_____

Culture note

What people think is beautiful changes over the years. For most of human history, heavier, rounder women were popular and fat men were seen as attractive because you had to be wealthy to be fat.

B. Vocabulary check: Fill in the crossword.

Across

2. It may not seem correct, but _____ it is.
7. He's strong and determined so he always does things in a _____ way.
8. We're starting to see the _____ of new forms of life.

Down

1. refuse
3. Something you do regularly becomes a _____ .
4. Don't _____ non-native species to this island.
5. The new diet is _____ .
6. Do you love ice cream? I _____ it.
9. a holy man

C. Choose the best answer.

1. *Patrons* refers to ___ .
   a. people who are saints
   b. people who support an organization or artist
   c. people who are customers
   d. people who insult you

2. Who was the first person to turn cocoa beans into something commercially important?
   a. Hernando Cortez
   b. Emperor Montezuma
   c. Christopher Columbus
   d. King Ferdinand

3. Chocolate, vanilla, cinnamon and chili pepper are examples of ___ .
   a. newly-discovered spices from Spain
   b. gifts offered in gold cups by Emperor Montezuma
   c. famous production houses in England
   d. agricultural treasures from the new continent

4. A synonym for *all the rage* is ___ .
   a. violent
   b. enjoyed
   c. angry
   d. popular

5. What has not changed since chocolate was first introduced?
   a. Adding sugar
   b. Making it liquid
   c. Adding milk
   d. Squeezing out cocoa butter

6. In line 5 in the second passage, *opposite* refers to ___ .
   a. we are lucky to live near the ocean
   b. we've stopped hunting, gathering and fishing
   c. we have plenty to eat
   d. we don't exercise enough

7. In line 22 in the second passage, *"little emperors"* refers to ___ .
   a. small children
   b. spoiled children
   c. young kings
   d. poor kings

8. In China, some parents and grandparents translate love and affection into ___ .
   a. making children exercise
   b. having fewer children
   c. giving children too much food
   d. lending greedy children money

Debate

Take one side, add your own ideas and debate in pairs or groups.

For: **Soon everyone in the world will be overweight.**
Points:

- In developed countries such as the United States, most people are overweight.

- There are too few opportunities for people to get exercise in their daily lives.

- Food is made too attractive through advertising.

- _____

- _____

- _____

Against: **Although some people eat too much, others do not.**
Points:

- Exercise is now more popular than ever.

- The media exaggerates weight problems.

- People may be overweight at different times of their lives, but not forever.

- _____

- _____

- _____

Debate strategy

When you debate, pay attention if your opponent uses a country as an example. If they say, "In the United States …," challenge him or her with the example of another country to throw the person off their argument.

Say:

- "Yes, well perhaps in the United States, but what about in (name of another country)?"
- "It may be true in the United States, but we're not in the U.S., are we?"

More ideas to debate

Enrico Caruso, ca. 1900s

Reading strategy

Proverbs are popular sayings that summarize a clever idea or small truth in one or two sentences.

"Watermelon—it's a good fruit. You eat, you drink, you wash your face."
Enrico Caruso (1873–1921) Opera singer

"The rich would have to eat money if the poor did not provide food."
Russian proverb

"The only way to keep your health is to eat what you don't want, drink what you don't like, and do what you'd rather not."
Mark Twain (1863–1910) Writer

"How can you govern a country which has 246 varieties of cheese?"
Charles de Gaulle (1890–1970) French leader

"There are four basic food groups: milk chocolate, dark chocolate, white chocolate and chocolate truffles."
Unknown

"Chocolate is a perfect food, as wholesome as it is delicious, a beneficent restorer of exhausted power. It is the best friend of those engaged in literary pursuits."
Baron Justus von Liebig (1803–1873) German chemist

Learn more

Food is a constant topic in the news because everyone has to have it. Find examples of issues about food in newspapers or on the WWW and report them to your class.

"She looks skinny to me. Yes, much too skinny!"

Look online

Check out the website at www.read-and-think.com for extra learning resources.

Add new words to your personal dictionary on page 176.

Marco Polo

Lesson One

Discussion

Before you read

- Who was Marco Polo and where did he go?
- What was life like in China and Europe during the 1200s?

Look at the map. What is different? What is the same?

An early map of the world

Reading strategy

When you read, you are always comparing
what is new to what you know. Look at
the old map and decide what doesn't fit
with what you know about the world.

Read about it

- Listen for comparisons using *like* and *as*.

The Travels of Marco Polo

Marco Polo (1254–1324) was born in Venice, Italy. His father, Niccolò Polo, was a businessman, so Marco was educated in business skills, as well as foreign languages.

Niccolò Polo and his brother, Marco's uncle Maffeo, made their money by traveling great distances to buy and sell goods. Their first Eastern journey was made in 1260, when Marco was still too young to go with them. From Venice, they traveled to the great city of Constantinople near the Black Sea, and from there made their way across parts of Russia to China, which was then ruled by Emperor Kublai Khan (1215–1294), grandson of Genghis Khan. In Beijing, the Emperor was delighted to meet them and hear their stories of faraway lands. After giving them expensive gifts, he sent them back to Europe with messages of peace for the Pope in Rome and requests for priests to teach him and his people more about Christianity. Kublai Khan also made them promise to return.

Marco Polo, fifteenth-century woodcut

The Polo brothers arrived back in Venice in 1269, and remained there for two years before deciding to return, mostly hoping to become as rich as kings. On

Reading strategy

When you read history, quickly scan the dates in the article first and get an idea of the general events being described. After you've read, make notes with the same dates, using a timeline.

The Polo brothers meet Kublai Khan, fourteenth-century painting

this second journey, they took Niccolò's son Marco, who was now seventeen
years old. On the journey back to Beijing, they took two priests to help teach
Kublai Khan about Christianity but, after entering countries in the midst of
civil war, the priests were as terrified as mice and scurried home. More
difficulties followed and the journey took three-and-a-half years. Finally, they
once again appeared before the Emperor. Kublai Khan was immediately
impressed with young Marco who became one of his favorites. The boy was
not only a good storyteller but he was also a quick learner, easily picking up
several dialects in both the Chinese and Mongol languages.

For seventeen years, the Polos remained in China and rose to posts of great
responsibility, for example, designing catapults to win the siege of Xianyang.
Marco was appointed a government official in the city of Yangzhou for three
years and undertook dangerous journeys for Kublai Khan throughout China
and as far as Burma and India. His favorite place in China was the city of
Hangzhou, famous for its twelve thousand bridges, but he was also greatly
impressed by Suzhou, with its canals like a Venice of the East. But finally, the
Polos decided it was time to leave before the old Emperor died. Kublai Khan
was sorry to see them go but let them travel with one last duty on their way
home: to deliver a princess to her new husband in Persia.

Computer note

It can be impossible
to find some places
in an atlas if you
only have the old
name, such as
Cathay for China.
Use the WWW to
search for places,
adding the word
"map" to your
search.

The trip was long and dangerous with sailors dying like flies—six hundred in all lost their lives to disease and pirate attacks. The Polos were lucky to make it home alive in 1295, and were so dirty and worn out that their own relatives could not recognize them. Fortunately, they had sewn countless precious jewels into their robes and were wealthy on their return to Venice. Four years later, when Marco Polo was captured and imprisoned after one of Venice's wars with Genoa, he dictated his adventures to another prisoner, a writer of romances called Rustichello of Pisa. The book of the travels became an immediate bestseller and brought great fame to Marco Polo.

When Marco Polo was old and ready to die, a priest came to his bedside and asked him about the many unbelievable stories he had told in his book. Did he want to admit his stories were all lies? Marco Polo shook his head and replied, "I have not told half of what I saw because no one would have believed me."

(607 words)

Reading strategy

When you come across long, new words, try to break them down to make them easier to understand: in the word *unbelievable*, *un-* means *not* and *-able* means *ability*.

Vocabulary notes

1. **admit** (verb) to agree unwillingly that something is true or that someone else is right
2. **appoint** (verb) to choose someone for a position or a job
3. **catapult** (noun) a large weapon used in former times to throw heavy stones, iron balls, etc.
4. **impress** (verb) to make someone feel admiration and respect
5. **imprison** (verb) to put someone in prison or to keep them somewhere and prevent them from leaving
6. **romance** (noun) a story about the love between two people
7. **sew** (verb) to use a needle and thread to make or repair clothes or to fasten something such as a button to them

Add new words to your personal dictionary on page 176.

Read and listen again to practice your pronunciation.

After you read

A. Answer these questions.

1. How old was Marco Polo when he traveled to China?
2. Who did Marco Polo meet in China?
3. What are two places Marco Polo visited in China?
4. Where was Marco Polo's wealth when he finally returned to Venice?
5. What did the priest want Marco Polo to admit?

Understand what you read

Similes

Unlike metaphors, which just say that one thing *is* another thing, similes are comparisons that are made using *like* or *as*. The comparisons can be of things or actions.

- *She swims like a fish.*
- *He eats like a pig.*
- *That dog is as big as a horse.*
- *It's as heavy as a ton of bricks.*

Here are four tips for working with similes:
- The idea of a simile is to give a feeling, not a precise description, for example, a ton is a ton, whether it's bricks or feathers, but bricks *sound* heavier.
- Usually there is only one part of the comparison that is meant to make sense. For example, if someone swims like a fish, the idea is ability.
- There are many well-known similes, such as those based on animal qualities, but not all are obvious. For example, c*razy like a fox* means *clever but only pretending to be crazy.*
- Different cultures admire different qualities in animals; the similes are not always easy to understand when translated.

B. Match the qualities to the animals to create similes.

1. blind as   a. a peacock

2. quiet as   b. a bat

3. brave as   c. an eel

4. slippery as   d. a lion

5. proud as   e. a mouse

C. Number the pictures in order according to the events in the passage.

D. Fill in the missing words. Use the correct form of the word.

- **carcass** (noun) the body of a dead animal
- **fallacious** (adjective) containing or based on false ideas
- **monstrous** (adjective) unusually large
- **preposterous** (adjective) completely unreasonable or silly
- **snatch** (verb) to take something away from someone with a quick, often violent, movement

Reading strategy

Focus on the general idea, not specific details, to improve your reading fluency. An easy way to do this is to skip the examples if you already understand.

Many have said amazing things about Marco Polo's discoveries. A _____ example is that he introduced pasta to Italy from China. Actually, pasta was already well-known long before Marco Polo was born. Some of his stories are clearly _____ . In one story, he describes a _____ bird, called a *roc*, that would _____ up an elephant, fly to great heights and then release it, to feast on its _____ .

What other parts of Marco Polo's stories are difficult to believe?

What about you?
Where in the world have you been? Where would you most like to go? Draw your travel plans on the map.

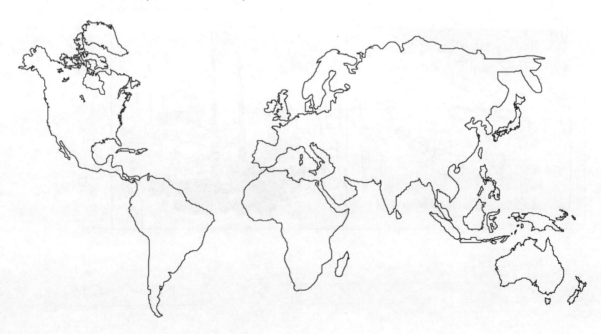

Lesson Two

Read about it

- What more do you learn in this article about Marco Polo?
- Which is more believable? Why?

A Million Lies

Marco Polo's *Travels*, or as it was originally called, *The Description of the World* or *The Travels of Marco Polo*, had an enormous impact when it was published. As it was published before the printing press, it was copied endlessly by hand. Mistakes in these copies meant that there are now around eighty "original" manuscript versions of *The Travels*. The book was also translated into many languages and became popular reading throughout Europe. After the invention of the printing press around 1454 by Johannes Gutenberg (1400–1468), *The Travels* became even more widely read.

From the time of its first publication, it was enormously influential. Other explorers and businessmen were inspired to take up dangerous journeys, philosophers and scholars debated life in distant China, and map makers started to redraw the world.

Calligraphy

There was only one problem: it was almost all lies. Even at the time it was published, the book was called *Il Milione,* or *The Million*, short for a million lies. Similarly, people called Marco Polo *Marco Milione*. At the time, these criticisms were understandable, because descriptions of life in a place as different as China would have been amazing to anyone in Europe. But more recently, people have examined the stories in the book one by one and compared them

77

Foot binding

to known facts. For example, an obvious error was the siege of Xianyang, which was already finished a year before the Polos were supposed to have arrived in China.

Another obvious error is the description of famous sights such as the bridges of Hangzhou; although Marco Polo claims there were more than twelve thousand, there are only about 360. Well, perhaps he could have made mistakes with his dates or counting, but what really disturbs most historians is what Marco Polo left out.

For example, if he was living in Beijing, it would have been almost impossible for him to have overlooked the Great Wall of China, but there is no mention of it. Why would he leave out a description of such an important feature? Similarly, he did not mention the practice of foot binding, where young girls' feet were tied with cloth to deform them and keep them from growing. Even more common was the Chinese practice of drinking tea, something that would have been

quite new in Europe. Nor did Marco Polo ever mention the art of Chinese calligraphy, which he would have presumably seen every day and may even have practiced himself.

But the major doubts about Marco Polo's accounts of his travels come from comparing what he said to Chinese historical records. Despite supposedly being a friend of the Emperor, his name and the names of his father and uncle are never mentioned in the *Annals of the Empire*, in the detailed records of the city of Yangzhou where Marco Polo was supposedly an important official, or anywhere else in Chinese records.

Then there are his descriptions of things and

The Great Wall

places in China. Although he claims to have learned several Mongol and Chinese dialects, he only ever uses the Persian words to describe Chinese things. This could be an important clue to the true story of Marco Polo's *Travels*.

What we do know is that Marco Polo's family did have a trading business based in Constantinople, and young Marco probably traveled there. He probably talked to lots of Persian businessmen, the "middle men" who would have met with Chinese traders in the desert and brought their goods to Constantinople. Many of the stories could have come from them.

Another possibility comes from common errors in spelling, history and geography in two other books, one by a Persian historian named Rashid al-Din published in 1310, and the other by a Chinese Buddhist historian, Nianchang, published in 1333. Although their stories are similar, it does not appear that any of these three authors could have read each other's work, so perhaps they all copied from another, now lost, book. Finding that book would be a real discovery!

(662 words)

Vocabulary notes

1. **calligraphy** (noun) the art of producing beautiful writing using special pens or brushes, or the writing produced this way
2. **deform** (verb) if you deform something, or if it deforms, its usual shape changes so that its usefulness or appearance is spoiled
3. **disturb** (verb) to make someone feel worried or upset
4. **historian** (noun) someone who studies history, or the history of a particular thing
5. **overlook** (verb) to not notice something, or not see how important it is
6. **presumably** (adverb) used to say that you think something is probably true
7. **supposedly** (adverb) used when saying what many people say or believe is true, especially when you disagree with them

 Read and listen again to practice your pronunciation.

Discussion

A. Summarize the main idea in one sentence.

"Man's perpetual curiosity regarding the unknown has opened many frontiers. Among the last to yield to the advance of scientific exploration has been the ocean floor. Until recent years much more was known about the surface of the moon than about the vast areas that lie beneath three-fourths of the surface of our own planet."

Submarine Geology (1948) by F.P. Shepard

B. Vocabulary check: Circle the words.

H	P	Z	U	I	M	P	R	I	S	O	N	E	A
B	R	T	D	Z	G	T	T	I	Q	W	H	D	R
T	E	R	I	I	Y	F	T	E	I	R	N	D	N
I	S	A	S	W	C	A	T	A	P	U	L	T	R
Y	U	N	T	A	C	C	O	U	A	D	M	I	T
U	M	S	U	S	U	P	P	O	S	E	D	L	Y
R	A	L	R	C	Q	B	R	H	J	F	K	L	W
O	B	A	B	S	A	V	I	M	P	R	E	S	S
M	L	T	N	Q	H	I	S	T	O	R	I	A	N
A	Y	E	J	B	S	N	A	T	C	H	I	N	H
N	H	D	S	V	S	A	P	P	O	I	N	T	E
C	O	V	E	R	L	O	O	K	E	D	S	X	Q
E	Q	X	W	O	S	C	U	R	R	I	E	D	P
S	O	C	A	L	L	I	G	R	A	P	H	Y	P

admit	calligraphy	imprison	romance	snatch
sew	catapult	overlook	impress	appoint
disturb	historian	presumably	supposedly	

C. Choose the best answer.

1. **What made Marco Polo popular with Kublai Khan?**
   a. His father was a traveler.
   b. Marco was a slow learner.
   c. Marco had blonde hair.
   d. Marco was a good storyteller.

2. **Which was not a request of Kublai Khan of the Polo brothers?**
   a. To give him rich gifts
   b. To deliver messages of peace
   c. To bring priests to him and his people
   d. To promise to return

3. ***The priests were as terrified as mice* is an example of ___ .**
   a. a metaphor
   b. a simile
   c. alliteration
   d. an idiom

4. **The author refers to Suzhou as *a Venice of the East* because both cities ___ .**
   a. have many many canals
   b. are in the East
   c. were Marco Polo's favorites
   d. required dangerous journeys to get there

5. **Who wrote *The Travels of Marco Polo*?**
   a. Marco Polo
   b. Maffeo Polo
   c. Kublai Khan
   d. Rustichello

6. ***"I have not told half of what I know because no one would have believed me."* Why would no one have believed Marco Polo?**
   a. People are naturally interested.
   b. The stories were too amazing.
   c. There were too many stories.
   d. The stories were lies.

7. **Mistakes were made in the first publications of *The Travels* because ___ .**
   a. the manuscript was too widely read
   b. copies were made by hand
   c. the original was not translated
   d. the stories were too long

8. **The interest of explorers, businessmen and philosophers shows ___ .**
   a. the influence of *The Travels of Marco Polo*
   b. the truth of *The Travels of Marco Polo*
   c. the lies of *The Travels of Marco Polo*
   d. the danger of *The Travels of Marco Polo*

Exam strategy

In multiple choice questions, some teachers take important or odd words from a reading and put them in the wrong answer. Think of what you know; don't be confused by what you don't know.

Debate

Take one side, add your own ideas and debate in pairs or groups.

For: There is still a lot of the world waiting to be discovered.

Points:
- Many places in the world have not been properly explored because they are hidden in jungles or mountains.

- Traces of ancient civilizations are waiting to be found.

- Exploring something new to you is still exploring, even if others have been there.

- _____

- _____

- _____

Against: The age of discovery is over.

Points:
- All of the world is already known and well-mapped.

- Satellites show us everything on the surface of the Earth.

- It's no longer possible to set off on a horse and find new places.

- _____

- _____

- _____

Debate strategy

When you debate, make sure you agree exactly about the topic of the debate. Sometimes your opponent may try to change the topic to suit his or her examples.

Say:
- "Excuse me, you seem to be talking about another topic."
- "How does this relate to the topic of ...?"
- "Perhaps we are not discussing the same thing. I understand the topic is ... but you are talking about ... ."

More ideas to debate

"In wisdom gathered over time I have found that every experience is a form of exploration."
Ansel Adams (1902–1984) Photographer

"America has been discovered before, but it has always been hushed up."
Oscar Wilde (1854–1900) Writer

"We shall not cease from exploration and the end of all our exploring will be to arrive where we started ... and know the place for the first time."
T.S. Eliot (1888–1965) Poet

"Writing is an exploration. You start from nothing and learn as you go."
E.L. Doctorow (1931–) Writer

Learn more

Who are some other great explorers? What did they discover? Find examples in the library or on the WWW and report them to your class.

Look online

Check out the website at www.read-and-think.com for extra learning resources.

Add new words to your personal dictionary on page 176.

Reading strategy

One way to check your reading comprehension is to read a sentence, such as one of these quotes, cover it, and try writing it out. Check the difference between what you read and what you write.

Mazes and Labyrinths

Lesson One

Before you read

- What is the difference between a maze and a labyrinth?
- What are mazes and labyrinths made from?

Trace the path through the maze.

A hedge maze, England

Language note

A view of something large from high above is usually called an *aerial view* or an *aerial photograph*.

- Listen for direction words.

Are You Lost?

Roman labyrinth

Almost everyone, at some time, has strolled along a labyrinth or through a maze. If not, they have probably traced a path through a maze on paper. A labyrinth is a twisted path; there is only one way to go and you have to follow it to the end. A maze is different; there are many paths and the usual intention of the maze designer is for you to get lost.   5

Labyrinths and mazes are among our oldest mysteries. The first ones we know about were created more than three thousand years ago and some of the same designs are found all over the world.

The materials and sizes of mazes and labyrinths are astonishingly varied. As decorations, they have been carved in rock, set on clay pots and tablets, 10 arranged with chipped colored stone in mosaics, woven into baskets and written on manuscripts. They have been built for people to walk through with walls of stone, wood, plants and other materials. In summer, huge mazes are created on farms with bales of hay. In winter, mazes are made from blocks of ice.   15

Reading strategy

It's much easier to understand this passage by looking at the diagrams than by reading the text. Before you read, quickly preview the diagrams to help you predict what the text will be about.

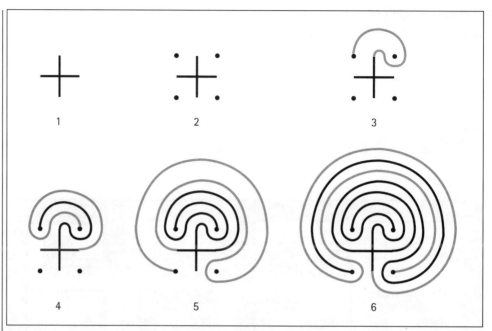

The seven-circuit labyrinth; start with a cross and four points, then join each line of the cross to the next point

The oldest and most common labyrinth design is called the *seven-circuit labyrinth* in which you walk clockwise and then counterclockwise at each circuit, getting closer and closer to the center. The design looks complicated but you can easily draw one if you know the trick. It involves starting with what is called a seed design and adding connecting lines in a set sequence from left to right. There are no written records of where the idea for the seven-circuit labyrinth came from. It is likely that the design was spread by travelers and then passed on from generation to generation. One curious coincidence is that the seven-circuit labyrinth is a map of the motion of the planet Mercury over a long period of time. Or maybe it is not a coincidence; perhaps ancient astronomers watched Mercury in the night sky and used its motion to make the first labyrinth designs. This might explain how the design became so popular around the world.

The labyrinth design was adopted by the Romans who used it to decorate their floors in colorful mosaics. It was further developed for use in medieval churches and cathedrals where examples are still found, often three to ten meters in diameter. People wander along these labyrinths as they pray.

Colonial Williamsburg maze

But the most famous labyrinth is one that no one has ever seen. It may never have existed. It was the labyrinth of the Minotaur.

The Minotaur was a monster that lived on the island of Crete where his father was king. King Minos and his wife offended the Greek gods and were punished. Minos' wife gave birth to a creature with the body of a man but the head and horns of a bull. King Minos imprisoned the Minotaur in a labyrinth where he fed it on young human victims. Fourteen victims were given annually as payment to King Minos by his enemy, King Aegeus of Athens, after Athens lost a war with Crete.

King Aegeus' son, Theseus, volunteered to be among the victims, thinking he could slay the Minotaur and end the suffering of Athens. He did so with the help of Ariadne, King Minos' daughter, who gave him string to trace his way back to where he started. However, this is a confusing part of the story. If Minotaur's lair was a labyrinth, there should have only been one way in and one way out. It was more likely a maze. But whatever was once there is now gone as King Minos' palace at Knossos burned to the ground sometime during the fifteenth century BC.

Today, labyrinths and mazes are more popular than ever. They are often built as tourist attractions where people can lose themselves—for fun.

(636 words)

Reading strategy

When reading myths, learn the names of the characters as they are often repeated in different stories. Make a family tree of the Greek and Roman gods to help you keep track of everyone.

1. **astronomer** (noun) a scientist who studies the stars and planets
2. **cathedral** (noun) the main church of a particular area under the control of a bishop
3. **diameter** (noun) a straight line from one side of a circle to the other side, passing through the center of the circle, or the length of this line
4. **labyrinth** (noun) a twisted path where there is only one way to go and you have to follow it to the end
5. **maze** (noun) a specially designed system of paths, often in a public park or garden, which is difficult to find your way through; a children's game on paper in which you try to draw a line through a complicated group of lines without crossing any of them
6. **mosaic** (noun) a pattern or picture made by fitting together small pieces of colored stone, glass, etc.
7. **slay** (verb) to kill someone

Add new words to your personal dictionary on page 176.

Read and listen again to practice your pronunciation.

A. Answer these questions.

1. What is the difference between a maze and a labyrinth?
2. What is a seed design?
3. Who might have invented the seven-circuit labyrinth?
4. What are mazes and labyrinths made from?
5. What did the Romans use to make decorative labyrinths?

Understand what you read

Sequence phrases

Writers often give directions for looking at something or describing something in a systematic way, starting from one point and moving toward another point. This helps the reader to see the words as a picture or even to direct attention to the important parts of a picture. The most common of these is the one that follows the direction we read, from left to right, and is used with things that are wide, while top to bottom are used with things that are tall. If there are a group of objects, pictures or items within a room, it's common to go clockwise (toward the right) or counterclockwise (toward the left). Objects with interior spaces might be described from the outside in or from the inside out.

Here are four tips for working with sequence phrases:
- Some sequence phrases begin with the most important thing.
- The purpose of sequence phrases is to create a picture in your mind. If you can't start to see a picture, start again.
- The phrase *working from* is often used to show the starting point of a direction.
- The phrase *moving on from* is often used between objects in a sequence.

Language note

Clockwise

Counterclockwise

Reading strategy

If a writer's way of describing a scene or object doesn't make sense to you, use your own direction words. The important thing is for you to have a good mental picture of what is being described.

B. Write direction phrases to describe:

1. the tallest building in the world
2. a theater stage with a symphony orchestra
3. the outside and inside of a volcano
4. a set of sculptures in a room of an art gallery
5. another person

C. Write the words in the correct order to make a limerick.

- fool, full A self-praise, of
- enter to decided maze a.
- big-headed very He was.
- we But, dreaded, as just
- for we seen haven't days him!

Language note

A limerick is a humorous short poem that has five lines that rhyme.

D. Fill in the missing words. Use the correct form of the word.

- **allegory** (noun) a story, painting, etc., in which the events and characters represent ideas or teach a moral lesson
- **exit** (verb) to leave a place
- **option** (noun) a choice you can make in a particular situation
- **passage** (noun) a journey on a ship
- **unaware** (adjective) not noticing or realizing what is happening

Mazes and labyrinths capture the imagination because they seem to be about much more than simply solving a puzzle or following a path. Instead, they are seen as an _____ for your _____ through life. Entering a maze is like starting off as a baby, _____ of what is to follow. As you journey through, you need to consider your _____ and make choices. Each choice leads you closer to the end of your life, where you _____ the maze, thinking about what you might have done if you had known more.

What other metaphors might a maze or labyrinth stand for?

What about you?

What kind of a maze would you like to design and what would you put inside it? Monsters? Treasures? Draw a maze below and add things for people to find.

Lesson Two

Read about it

- Who were Theseus and the Minotaur?
- What is the importance of promises in this play?

Forgotten Promises

Characters

King Aegeus
Prince Theseus
Princess Ariadne
5 Minotaur

Act I

In Athens, at the court of King Aegeus, the old King is crying. Prince Theseus, wearing a smaller crown, enters. He is
10 *disturbed to see his father upset. Distant drums are beating.*

Theseus slaying the Minotaur

Theseus: Father, what is it? Why are you crying?
Aegeus: It is the drums, Theseus. The drums
15 are calling together the young people of Athens. Soon another fourteen will be selected.
Theseus: Selected? Selected for what? I don't understand, Father.
20 **Aegeus:** I should begin at the beginning.

Long ago, our kingdom fought that of Minos, King of Crete. We lost, and he was able to choose whatever payment he wanted.
Theseus: Any payment? You mean all your gold?
25 **Aegeus:** Worse. He wanted our young people. Each year, fourteen young people must be selected by lot. They set sail on the next boat to Crete.
Theseus: But why? Does King Minos want
30 them for slaves?
Aegeus: No. It would be much better if they

91

were slaves. Then at least they might someday be free and return to their parents in Athens. But a much worse fate awaits them.

Theseus: What could that be?

Aegeus: The Minotaur.

Theseus: I've heard stories about the Minotaur, but I did not believe he really exists.

Aegeus: He does. He is a huge monster, half man with the head of a bull. And he hungers for human flesh. The fourteen who go to him go to their deaths.

Theseus: But this can't be allowed to happen!

Aegeus: I'm afraid there's no choice. While the Minotaur lives, we must each year send seven young men and seven young women.

Theseus: Then the Minotaur must live no more! I shall go, Father. I shall go and kill the Minotaur.

Aegeus: But you would only perish like the rest.

Theseus: *(laughs)* Trust me, Father. I shall return in victory.

Aegeus: If you must go, then promise me this. The ship that takes you to Crete has black sails and white sails. If the ship returns with bad news, it will use its black sails to tell me of your death. If by chance you defeat the Minotaur and escape, put up the white sails and I will be at the dock to welcome you home.

Theseus: I promise, Father. Now, I must go!

Act II

A moonlit night in King Minos' palace. A young woman carrying a candle creeps forward to where Theseus is sleeping.

Theseus: Wait! Who are you?

Ariadne: Sh. It is me, Ariadne. *(She comes closer to where he can see her.)* Be quiet or you'll wake the guards.

Theseus: I saw you this afternoon. You were with the King.

Ariadne: King Minos is my father.

Theseus: Tomorrow he plans to feed us to the Minotaur. He's a cruel man.

Ariadne: I think he's cruel, too. And I want to escape from here as much as you do.

Theseus: Why are you telling me this?

Ariadne: I want to help you. And I want you to help me.

Theseus: How?

Ariadne: I know the secret of the labyrinth. Here is a dagger. If you go in now, you can kill the Minotaur while he is sleeping.

Theseus: But how will I find my way out again?

Ariadne: With this golden ball of string. Tie it to the entrance and find your way back.

Theseus: And in return?

Ariadne: And in return, promise to take me with you when you go.

Theseus: I promise.

Ariadne: Remember, you must always keep your promises.

Act III

Theseus in the labyrinth carefully ties his 100
string and walks around in circles until he
finds the sleeping Minotaur in the center of
the stage. He takes out his dagger to kill him
but foolishly makes a sound. The Minotaur
wakes and they struggle. Finally, he kills the 105
Minotaur and retraces his steps with the
string.

Act IV

On the ship bound for Athens. Black sails
are hoisted. 110

Theseus: OK, this is far enough. I will set
you down on this island.

Ariadne: But you have forgotten your
promise!

Theseus: No, I only promised to take you 115
away and ... oh, no!

Ariadne: What now?

Theseus: My promise to my father. I meant
to change the sails to white ... .

Ariadne: Listen. 120

(sounds of distant screams)

Ariadne: The women of Athens are
mourning. Your father has seen the sails and
killed himself. You are cursed for forgetting
your promises. 125

(Darkness falls.)

(738 words)

Vocabulary notes

1. **dagger** (noun) a short pointed knife used as a weapon
2. **dock** (noun) a place in a port where ships are loaded, unloaded or repaired
3. **lot** (noun) if someone is chosen by lot, several people each take a piece of paper or an object from a container, and the person who is chosen is the one who gets a particular marked paper or object
4. **mourn** (verb) to feel very sad and to miss someone after they have died
5. **perish** (verb) to die, especially in a terrible or sudden way
6. **retrace** (verb) to go back exactly the way you have come
7. **victory** (noun) the success you achieve when you win a battle, game, election, etc.

Reading strategy

Plays are written to be spoken, so it helps to read them aloud, even if you are only by yourself. In this way, you can sometimes better understand the rhythm of the language.

Read and listen again to practice your pronunciation.

After you read

A. Summarize the main idea in one sentence.

A *protagonist* is the person in a play that you identify with. Usually, the protagonist is not perfect. Theseus does a great thing (slaying the Minotaur) but forgets a small detail (changing the sails). This mixture of qualities makes him more interesting for us. The opposite of protagonist is *antagonist*.

_____

B. Vocabulary check: Circle the words.

B	S	I	I	U	I	M	O	S	A	I	C	S	R	S
J	Y	D	A	G	G	E	R	R	A	U	S	C	L	I
I	P	S	L	M	S	S	S	I	L	M	H	Y	O	S
S	P	H	L	A	D	I	D	M	I	M	I	I	T	A
Y	E	F	E	R	O	I	S	C	C	A	I	I	N	I
B	R	W	G	I	C	B	R	I	I	Z	I	R	B	S
O	I	T	O	S	K	A	U	S	A	E	S	L	A	Y
A	S	T	R	O	N	O	M	E	R	A	B	I	S	M
F	H	I	Y	L	S	H	Y	I	I	A	C	E	L	I
G	I	P	A	S	S	A	G	E	I	N	S	X	I	B
S	R	D	I	A	M	E	T	E	R	I	S	I	O	I
O	L	A	B	Y	R	I	N	T	H	P	C	T	W	I
W	I	I	L	S	H	Y	P	S	O	P	T	I	O	N

allegory	diameter	labyrinth	mosaic	perish
astronomer	dock	lot	option	slay
dagger	exit	maze	passage	

Culture note

Arthur Evans (1851–1941) went to Crete in 1894 and discovered Knossos, the legendary city of the palace of King Minos. However, he did not discover the labyrinth of the Minotaur.

C. Choose the best answer.

1. The difference between a maze and a labyrinth is that ___ .
   a. a maze has no paths that you have to follow to the end
   b. a labyrinth has only one path that you follow to the end
   c. a maze has one path to get lost in
   d. a labyrinth has many paths to get lost in

2. Mazes and labyrinths have not been built for ___ .
   a. churches
   b. decoration
   c. fun
   d. cemeteries

3. The phrase *trace a path* means ___ .
   a. outline or follow with a pencil
   b. walk along a single lane road
   c. copy a line using translucent paper
   d. find the remains of a former walkway

4. A theory for the spread of the seven-circuit labyrinth is that ___ .
   a. travelers took the idea with them
   b. astronomers from Mercury shared them
   c. Romans took them to Brazil
   d. King Minos gave tours of his labyrinth

5. What is interesting about the most famous labyrinth?
   a. No one has seen it and it may never have existed.
   b. People wandered along it to pray.
   c. It was made from hay in the summer and ice in the winter.
   d. People lost themselves in it for fun.

6. Why is King Aegeus crying at the beginning of Act I?
   a. His son will die.
   b. The Minotaur will die.
   c. Young people will die.
   d. The King will die.

7. The ultimate result of the King of Crete's demand will be that ___ .
   a. the gold of Athens will eventually run out
   b. young Athenians will always live in fear
   c. the King of Athens will eventually lose his throne
   d. the ships of Athens will eventually all sail under black sails

8. A synonym for *hoisted* is ___ .
   a. torn
   b. lowered
   c. raised
   d. fixed

Debate

Take one side, add your own ideas and debate in pairs or groups.

For: A maze is a good metaphor for life.

Points:

- A maze has a beginning, a middle and an end.

- We all start on the same path in life, but make different choices.

- People who seem to take an easy way in life, aren't always happiest.

- _____

- _____

- _____

Against: A maze is not a good metaphor for life.

Points:

- We are all born with different advantages to help us through life.

- We can take advantage of others' knowledge to predict trouble and offer help.

- Not everyone lives the same length of time.

- _____

- _____

- _____

Debate strategy

When you debate, don't leave a question unanswered if you know the answer. If you don't know the answer, you can shift the topic.

Say:

- "That's an interesting question, but we are really talking about ... ."

Another idea to debate

"Happiness, that grand mistress of the ceremonies in the dance of life, impels us through all its mazes and meanderings, but leads none of us by the same route."
Charles Caleb Colton (1780–1832) Writer

Learn more

It's easy to find examples of mazes and labyrinths in the library or on the WWW. Find examples and report them to your class. Try to design a maze yourself.

Reading strategy

Human qualities are often described in similes and metaphors. Although the descriptions may sound simple and attractive, be careful that they don't use faulty logic.

Look online

Check out the website at www.read-and-think.com for extra learning resources.

Add new words to your personal dictionary on page 176.

Let's Play a Game!

Lesson One

Before you read

- How often do you play games?
- What do you like to play?

Do you know how to play this game?

A student playing a game of go

Reading strategy

Questions often give clues, as do pictures. You know this is a game and the boy is Asian, so you might guess it is an Asian game.

Read about it

- Listen for examples where something is suggested, without being said.

Chess

Chess pieces

Chess is an ancient game. No one knows exactly where it first came from, but the earliest form of chess is probably *shaturanga*, which was invented in India sometime before 600 AD by an Indian philosopher. The philosopher was supposedly asked by a cruel *raja*, or king, to find a way to end war. To make the philosopher think harder, the king gave him a month and told him he would be killed if he failed. The philosopher nodded and went back to his house. All day long he sat in the sun carving pieces of wood into one figure after another. At the end of a month, he returned to the king with a board game where kings and armies could fight without anyone dying. The king was delighted with the game and told the philosopher he could have anything he wanted.

The philosopher said he wanted nothing for himself, but asked for one grain of rice to be put on the first square of the board and then be doubled on each consecutive square—two, four, eight, etc. The king should give the rice on the sixty-fourth square to the poor. The king laughed and told the philosopher he was foolish to ask for so little. But how many grains of rice was it? Draw a chessboard, eight squares by eight squares, and write out the numbers.

This early form of chess was a battle between four armies, each controlled by a king. Each army included four pawns, a ship, an elephant and a horse. Four people played, on two teams. The board was the same one of sixty-four squares we use today, but was based on an earlier racing game, *ashtapada*.

The biggest difference between *shaturanga* and modern chess was that dice were used to decide which piece went next—each piece had its own number. The use of dice added chance. And where there is chance, people like to gamble. Gambling on *shaturanga* became quite popular. Laws were passed in India to stop people from gambling so *shaturanga* players simply stopped using dice. Around this time, someone decided to merge the pieces into two armies so the game could be played by just two people. A few other changes were made to the moves each piece could make and the new game was called *shatranj*.

This new game is first mentioned in 600 AD, in a book which says an Indian ambassador traveled to Persia around that time. The ambassador gave a *shatranj* game as a gift to the king, and challenged him to learn its secrets. The game became popular and, within fifty years, spread to Arab kingdoms and as far as Greece.

There are several stories about how the game spread through the rest of the world. One says it was brought to Europe by Arabs traveling through Spain. Another says European travelers to the Arab kingdoms brought the game back.

Another story says that the European ruler Charlemagne (742–814) and the Empress Irene (752–803) of the Byzantine Empire once considered getting married. It would have been a good political move to unite large parts of the world. During one of their meetings, Empress Irene gave Charlemagne a *shatranj* set. But the game had a new twist; it included two queens and they were the most

Two dice

Reading strategy

When more than one version of a story or explanation is given, pay attention to how the writer signals what he or she thinks is the most important or likely one; often, it is the last one mentioned.

powerful pieces on the board. Charlemagne thought this might be a bad sign and decided that the marriage wasn't such a good idea after all!

From Northern India, chess spread to Burma where it is still played in an interesting way: each player chooses where to arrange his or her pieces on the board. Chinese, Japanese and Korean chess games are all modern forms of *shatranj*.

Today, chess pieces come in many beautiful designs but, in the early 1700s, they were either rough wooden pieces used by the poor or impractical, highly-decorated pieces used by the rich. In 1847, the modern designs of chess sets were created, improved on slightly by 1890, and have been used in the same form ever since.

(670 words)

60

65

Reading strategy

Many stories are apocryphal, that is, they may not be true. The story about Charlemagne depends on what he thought, but as he never learned to write, we don't know if it really happened.

Vocabulary notes

1. **chance** (noun) how possible or likely it is that something will happen, especially something that you want
2. **dice** (noun) small blocks of wood, plastic, etc., that have six sides with a different number of spots on each side, used in games
3. **gambling** (noun) when people risk money or possessions on the result of something that is not certain, such as a card game or a horse race
4. **impractical** (adjective) not sensible or possible for practical reasons
5. **merge** (verb) to combine, or to join things together to form one thing
6. **piece** (noun) a small object used in a game such as chess
7. **twist** (noun) an unexpected feature or change in a situation or series of events

Add new words to your personal dictionary on page 176.

Read and listen again to practice your pronunciation.

After you read

A. Answer these questions.

1. Where was chess first invented?
2. Why did Charlemagne change his mind about marrying Empress Irene?
3. Why did dice disappear from chess?
4. Why might the philosopher have invented chess?
5. When were modern chess pieces invented?

Understand what you read

Inference

Inferences are guesses, made on the basis of what is or is not mentioned. You understand much about what you read and hear by making inferences. For example, from the sentence, *She blew out the candles and served the cake.* we can infer that a girl or woman is having her birthday party with other people, even though the sentence doesn't mention these things.

Here are four tips for working with inferences:
- Inferences are used extensively in both fiction and non-fiction.
- Inferences usually depend on understanding the context of the conversation.
- Understanding inferences is easier when you know the different meanings of words. The sentence, *Mary had a fish dish.* could mean that Mary ate fish in a restaurant, but if Mary were in a pottery shop, it might mean that she was holding a bowl with a fish on it or that the bowl was in the shape of a fish.
- Inferences are sometimes necessary and expected when someone doesn't want to say or write about something unpleasant, for example, *He died in a car crash last night after leaving a bar at 3:00 in the morning.* suggests that a man had an accident because he had had too much to drink at a bar, possibly because he was there so late.

B. Read and explain the inference.

1. I met John and Sally. Sally is nice.
2. I'm not sure you understand. You're quite young.
3. Either you go to university or you'll never get a job.
4. Paris is beautiful, if you like old buildings.
5. Everyone loves Peter because he's so kind.

102

C. Number the sentences.

___ By doubling the number of grains of rice on each square, the number quickly increases.

___ For example, in just the first row, the grains increase from 1 to 2, 4, 8, 16, 32, 64, 128.

___ On the last square of the board, the number has reached approximately 9,200,000,000,000,000,000 grains of rice. (Say, *9.2 quintillion.*)

___ That's a lot of rice!

___ The king thought that the philosopher was stupid, but it was the other way around.

___ This is the reason why.

___ This may not seem much, but by the end of the second row, the number is already 32,768.

Language note

Many differences between British English and American English can be confusing. A British billion is a million million (1,000,000,000,000), but an American billion is a thousand million (1,000,000,000)–quite a difference!

D. Fill in the missing words. Use the correct form of the word.

- **adventurous** (adjective) not afraid of taking risks or trying new things
- **constant** (adjective) happening regularly or all the time
- **dynamic** (adjective) continuously moving or changing
- **flair** (noun) a natural ability to do something very well
- **static** (adjective) not moving, changing or developing

"To be creative, to be _____ , to exhibit _____ , is no excuse for not studying hard. The truth is exactly the opposite. You have to work constantly at your game, at your openings and endings. A deep analysis is necessary. Chess is not a fixed or _____ body of knowledge. It's _____ . Even the books I've written on chess and the annotations I've made on my own matches are not set in stone. I keep updating them. There must be a _____ questioning of old ideas, even one's own."

Garry Kasparov (1963–) Chess grand master

Which of the above qualities are also true for a good student?
What are other qualities of a good student?

Reading strategy

Repetition is an important tool in writing. It's used for emphasis, often repeating the same idea in several but similar ways. When you see repetition, be aware that the writer thinks the idea is particularly important.

Lesson Two

- What are online games?
- What is an addiction?

The Girl in Gray

Mrs. Kim did not want to do it, but she finally had no choice. She had not seen her daughter Nancy for six weeks or, rather, Nancy had
5 not seen her.

Nancy was seventeen and spent all her time sitting in her room at her computer, playing online games
10 with teenagers exactly like her. If Mrs. Kim touched the beeping, buzzing computer or pulled the plug, Nancy
15 flew into a rage. "If you try that again, I'll, I'll ...!" she shouted. But even as she said the words, her eyes
20 were turning back toward the glowing screen. After a few

months, Mrs. Kim began to notice that Nancy did not care about eating anymore. She started feeding her
25 daughter by hand and giving her drinks by putting a straw in her mouth. The addiction was a nightmare, a terrible nightmare. Many parents said

it was the same problem with their children. Then Mr. Tan, the man who sold newspapers, told Mrs. Kim about User Reprogram Co. "It's too expensive for me," Mr. Tan said. "And you have to sign a form that lets them do anything necessary to get your child away from the computer. Anything. But they guarantee they will do it."

So, one Monday morning, Mrs. Kim found herself sitting in the gray offices of User Reprogram Co. At a gray desk in front of her sat a smiling girl wearing a gray uniform. Behind her, were hundreds of other girls just like her, in gray uniforms at gray desks. None of the desks had computers on them. The girl was not much older than Nancy. But there was something not quite right about her ... she seemed to smile a little too much. All the other girls were smiling, too.

The girl didn't seem too interested in hearing about Nancy. She just smiled, nodded and pushed the form at Mrs. Kim. "Don't lock your door tonight," she explained. "We'll come when you're sleeping."

Mrs. Kim went home to feed Nancy. She saw Nancy's score was now over ten billion. She did as the girl asked and went to bed. Sometime in the night, she thought she heard the front door open and close.

When Mrs. Kim got up the next morning, it seemed nothing had changed. Nancy was still sitting at the computer. She usually fell asleep there and started playing again as soon as she woke up. But something was different. On the screen, in one corner, was a small figure in gray. It was the girl from User Reprogram Co. She was smiling.

Language note

The abbreviations *Co.* and *Ltd.* are usually pronounced *company* and *limited*. The abbreviation *Inc.* is pronounced *incorporated* or sometimes just *ink.*

"Someone must have come in to tamper with Nancy's computer without her knowing," Mrs. Kim thought to herself. She said nothing. As the days went by, Mrs. Kim began to see a few small changes. First, the smiling girl on the screen was getting a little larger—and she was whispering something; Mrs. Kim couldn't quite hear. Second, Nancy's score had not changed much; she was no longer adding up points by the thousand.

By the end of the week, the games still played on but Nancy could hardly bother to lift her fingers to the keyboard. By the end of the week, the girl in gray had grown on the screen so that now her smiling face filled it. She was still whispering but, curiously, when Mrs. Kim came closer, she seemed to stop.

One morning, ten days after she had visited User Reprogram Co., Mrs. Kim woke up suddenly. Something was terribly wrong, but what was it? She listened but she couldn't hear a thing. Then she understood; for the first time in years, she couldn't hear the computer. She quickly got out of bed and went to Nancy's room. Not only was the computer off, but Nancy was standing there, neatly dressed, putting on her coat.

"Nancy!" Mrs. Kim cried. "What are you doing?"

"Good morning, Mom." she replied. "I've had enough of computers. I'm going to get a job."

"Well, that's wonderful," Mrs. Kim said. "Tonight I will make a special dinner and we can ... ." But Nancy had already walked out the door.

When Nancy didn't come home for dinner, Mrs. Kim was disappointed but not worried. When she didn't come home that night, Mrs. Kim was worried. In the morning, when she still wasn't there, Mrs. Kim was desperate and ran down to the offices of User Reprogram Co. She pushed past the other parents and, just as she thought, in a far corner of the room, she saw Nancy. She was sitting in a gray uniform at a gray desk. She was smiling.

(769 words)

Reading strategy

Short stories are seldom completely finished. Usually, you are expected to add your own ideas about what happens next. What do you think happens next in this story?

Vocabulary notes

1. **addiction** (noun) a strong desire to do or have something regularly
2. **bother** (verb) to make the effort to do something
3. **guarantee** (verb) to make it certain that something will happen
4. **notice** (verb) if you notice something or someone, you realize that they exist, especially because you can see, hear or feel them
5. **score** (noun) the number of points that each team or player has won in a game or competition
6. **straw** (noun) a thin tube of paper or plastic for sucking up liquid from a bottle or a cup
7. **tamper** (verb) to touch something or make changes to it without permission

Read and listen again to practice your pronunciation.

After you read

A. Summarize the main idea in one sentence.

Traditional board games, such as chess, continue to be as popular as ever. But new types of games are also being developed using virtual-reality tools. Computer games will soon allow people to make models of themselves and put them into adventures involving other people. You will wear a special suit so that the figure on screen will follow your movements and will say the words you say. But unlike life, you will always be able to start over.

B. Vocabulary check: Fill in the crossword.

Across

1. a surprising development
3. constantly changing
7. a promise
9. a small object used in games
10. something for adding chance to games
11. putting two things together

Down

2. The person with the most points has the highest _____ .
4. pay attention
5. opportunity for the unexpected
6. playing for money
8. The thief will _____ with the alarm system.

C. Choose the best answer.

1. Mrs. Kim feeds her daughter ___ .
   a. so they can have dinner together
   b. so she doesn't stop eating and die
   c. because she's too young to feed herself
   d. because she likes chocolates

2. Nancy has an addiction to ___ .
   a. wine
   b. candy
   c. magazines
   d. computer games

3. We can infer that Nancy has no ___ .
   a. computer
   b. mother
   c. father
   d. workers

4. The girls in gray smile ___ .
   a. to be polite
   b. because they aren't in control of themselves
   c. because they are scared
   d. only at night

5. Everything is gray in the story because ___ .
   a. it's a dull color
   b. they couldn't get red
   c. it's better than black and white
   d. it's the last color you think about

6. The story *The Girl in Gray* ___ .
   a. is mostly about girls
   b. is really about boys
   c. could apply to both girls and boys
   d. isn't about boys or girls

7. The theme of *The Girl in Gray* is:
   a. How to get rid of your daughter
   b. Solutions can be worse than problems
   c. Loving computer games
   d. Getting help for your problems

8. The girl on the screen may stop talking because ___ .
   a. the computer is broken
   b. the face is broken
   c. Nancy turns it off
   d. it doesn't want Mrs. Kim to hear

9. At the end of the story, Nancy ___ .
   a. has been tricked into working for the company
   b. is working at a computer store
   c. gets her own apartment
   d. begins to write her own games

10. At the end of the story, Mrs. Kim ___ .
    a. wants to learn computing
    b. goes out with some other parents
    c. finds someone else for Nancy's room
    d. wants to get her daughter back

Exam strategy

When writing your answer, don't bother rewriting the question as part of your answer. It's a waste of time for you and the teacher. Just *answer* the question.

Debate

Take one side, add your own ideas and debate in pairs or groups.

For: Games are a great way to pass the time.	*Against:* Games are a waste of time.

Points:
- Games are social and let you meet and enjoy time with other people.

- Games teach skills of strategy and making the most of chance.

- Many games encourage your mathematical skills.

- _____

- _____

- _____

Points:
- Games are just a way of making people feel more important than they are.

- Being good at a game doesn't make you good at life.

- The same time spent with a book would be more useful.

- _____

- _____

- _____

Debate strategy

When you debate, challenge the inferences your opponent makes. For example, if a person infers that you just don't understand, make it clear that you do.

Say:
- "My opponent is trying to infer that I don't understand, but I do. More importantly, she does not understand that ... ."

More ideas to debate

"People's affections can be as thin as paper; life is like a game of chess, changing with each move."
Chinese proverb

"Chess is the gymnasium of the mind."
Vladimir Lenin (1870–1924) Russian leader

"If you're too busy to play chess ... you're too busy."
Unknown

"I once heard of a murderer who propped his two victims up against a chessboard in sporting attitudes and was able to get as far as Seattle before his crime was discovered."
Robert Benchley (1889–1945) Writer

"Life's too short for chess."
Henry J. Byron (1834–1884) Dramatist

Think about it

Benchley's quote is a joke that depends on an inference about how people play chess. What is the inference?

Learn more

You probably know the names of many games but don't know how to play them. Find the rules of a new game and report them to your class.

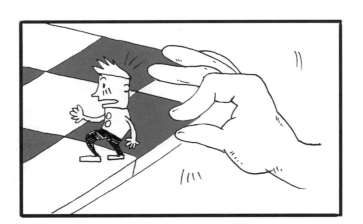

Look online

Check out the website at www.read-and-think.com for extra learning resources.

Add new words to your personal dictionary on page 176.

Ang Lee

Lesson One

Before you read

- Who is Ang Lee?
- What is a trilogy?

What things in the picture suggest another time?

Scene from *Sense and Sensibility*, directed by Ang Lee

Reading strategy

When you look at a historical picture or period scene, compare how the same scene would look today. Is this how people picnic in the twenty-first century?

- Listen for examples of conflict.

Making Movies

One of the most successful filmmakers today doesn't live in Hollywood and isn't married to a movie star. He doesn't make just one kind of film and he doesn't work in just one language. He doesn't just direct movies, he writes and produces them as well. His name is Ang Lee.

Ang Lee was born in 1954 in Taiwan. He came from a family of scholars. His [5] father, a school principal, fled the People's Republic of China after his parents were executed for being landlords. Rather than follow an intellectual life, Lee decided to study acting. He graduated from the National Taiwan College of Arts in 1975 and then went to the United States, where he studied directing (for theater) at the University of Illinois, and film production at New York [10] University. In New York, he worked with other student filmmakers such as Spike Lee and made his own short movies, including *Dim Lake* (1983) and *Fine Line* (1984).

These prize-winning short movies were enough for Lee to get accepted for representation by the [15] William Morris Talent Agency but, despite considerable hard work, five years went by when his only starring role [20] was as a house husband, taking care of his two sons. His wife, research microbiologist Janice Lin, supported the [25]

Ang Lee, with cast members of *Eat Drink Man Woman*

His big break finally came as a surprise. In 1990, Lee entered two scripts into a national competition in Taiwan. Amazingly, the scripts managed to take first and second place. *Pushing Hands* (1991) and *The Wedding Banquet* (1993) were later joined by *Eat Drink Man Woman* (1994), as a set of three loosely connected films that Lee called his "Father Knows Best" trilogy, all featuring the fatherly actor Sihung Lung.

Pushing Hands

The father in *Pushing Hands* is a *tai chi* master who leaves his native Beijing to retire in New York, hoping to spend his last years with his only son, who is married to a tense, non-Chinese writer. Unfortunately, everything her father-in-law tries to do to help inadvertently upsets her. Problems in communication between cultures are a source of much of the movie's bittersweet humor. And although he has spent his entire life seeking harmony from *tai chi*, the father cannot seem to achieve it in his new home.

However, the movie is a comedy and he is eventually rescued by romance. The movie is slightly autobiographical, based on Lee's own loneliness when he first moved away from home to study in the United States.

The Wedding Banquet

The father in the second movie, *The Wedding Banquet*, is a stern retired general who, along with his wife, has been pressuring their only son, Gao Wai, to marry and have children. There is just one problem: Gao is gay and is already in a serious long-term relationship with another

Gao marries Wei Wei in *The Wedding Banquet*

man. Finally, he finds a compromise. Wei Wei, a young artist, needs to marry an American just to get citizenship. Otherwise she will have to leave the country. Their simple marriage of convenience with a quiet ceremony at City Hall becomes complicated when Gao's parents arrive and a giant wedding banquet is arranged.

Language note

Prefixes that tell you about numbers are *uni-*, *bi-*, *tri-*, *quad-* and *quin-*, which refer to 1, 2, 3, 4 and 5, respectively. Learning these can help you understand many new words.

Eat Drink Man Woman

The father in the third movie of the trilogy is a famous Taiwanese chef and widower. Every week, he prepares a banquet for his three adult daughters. The movie opens with mouth-watering preparations for this banquet. Ironically, however, despite his fame, he has recently lost his sense of taste

Dinner is served in *Eat Drink Man Woman*

and the beautiful food tastes terrible. As the movie unfolds, each of the characters changes his or her situation in surprising ways.

In exploring the different and changing roles of a father, the three films also look at problems between generations, each not understanding the other. Another theme is the way in which food brings people together. Perhaps it is a lesson Ang Lee learned in his five years at home making meals for his wife and children.

(670 words)

Reading strategy

Film reviews usually leave out the ending of the film. Instead, they try to give the reader a general idea of the plot and theme. When you read a review, try to predict what will happen next.

Vocabulary notes

1. **bittersweet** (adjective) feelings, memories, or experiences that are bittersweet are happy and sad at the same time
2. **gay** (adjective) if someone, especially a man, is gay, they are sexually attracted to people of the same sex
3. **generation** (noun) all people of about the same age
4. **harmony** (noun) the pleasant effect made by different things that form an attractive whole
5. **inadvertently** (adverb) without realizing what you are doing
6. **script** (noun) the written form of a speech, play, film, etc.
7. **star** (verb) if someone stars in a film, television show, etc., they are one of the main characters in it
8. **trilogy** (noun) a series of three plays, books, etc., that are about the same people or subject

Add new words to your personal dictionary on page 176.

Read and listen again to practice your pronunciation.

A. Answer these questions.

1. Where did Ang Lee train to become a director?
2. What is the subject of Ang Lee's trilogy?
3. How is *Pushing Hands* autobiographical?
4. What purpose does food have in his trilogy?
5. What is the irony in *Eat Drink Man Woman*?

Understand what you read

Conflict in fiction

Whether in books or movies, one of the most important things in any story is the conflict. There are normally four types of conflict:

a. a person fighting against another person
b. a person fighting against nature
c. a person fighting against society
d. a person fighting against himself or herself

Here are four tips for understanding conflict:

- Different forms of conflict can be mixed up, with more than one happening at the same time.
- A person fighting against himself or herself is often seen in the form of having to make a difficult decision.
- Conflicts can change over the course of a movie or novel. What starts out as escaping a forest fire may turn into a struggle between two people.
- Conflicts end in a *resolution*, an event or decision that restores balance.

B. Match these examples to the type of conflict.

1. _____ A prince thinks he sees his father's ghost and has to decide whether or not to follow its advice to kill someone.

2. _____ A volcano is about to erupt and a woman has two hours to save a town.

3. _____ Two boys love the same girl and compete to impress her.

4. _____ A plane crashes and the survivors struggle to survive on a desert island.

5. _____ An explorer discovers a primitive civilization and is horrified by their practice of killing ten young women for the Moon god.

C. Read and circle the correct words.

Despite mostly working on Chinese language films, Ang Lee was (hired / fired) to direct a film adapted by Emma Thompson from Jane Austen's classic novel, *Sense and Sensibility*. Most critics (were / were not) surprised at the choice and even Lee found the first days of filming very (easy / difficult). While he was used to making all the decisions and having them carried out promptly, he found that the British film-making style lets everyone (take / give) an opinion. However, the film was an immediate success and critics (found / lost) many (differences / similarities) between it and Lee's earlier films. For example, it's about the effect of a father on his family and the problems of miscommunication.

Language note

When you are looking for *conflict* in a story, look for synonyms, for example, *argument, battle, clash, disagreement, fight, quarrel, struggle* and *war*.

Reading strategy

After you read, make a note about the conflict and resolution to help you remember the plot. Many stories share a common plot.

D. Fill in the missing words. Use the correct form of the word.

- **convention** (noun) a method or style often used in literature, art, the theater, etc., to achieve a particular effect
- **exceptional** (adjective) unusual and likely not to happen often
- **suspend disbelief** (verb) to try to believe that something is true, for example when you are watching a film or play
- **sync** (noun) if things are in sync, they are working well together at exactly the same time and speed
- **voice-over** (noun) information or remarks that are spoken on a television program or film by someone who is not seen on the screen

When we watch a movie, we almost always _____ and accept many things that would confuse someone who had never seen a movie before. These _____ in movies include frequent switches in time and place and the use of music to add emotion to a scene. In Indian movies, it's not _____ for a woman to walk into a room in one beautiful outfit then a second later be seen in the same scene in another outfit. She might look out one window and see the mountains of the north of India and look out another and see a beach, several thousand kilometers to the south. _____ are another odd feature of some movies in which lips seldom match what is being said. But, in Italy, this is so common that movies made in Italian sometimes purposely have the speech and lips out of _____ to make them feel foreign.

Reading strategy

In this unit, there are many two-part words that are easy to understand if you know the words that make them up: *prize-winning, self-taught, long-term*. Make a list of others you find.

What about you?
Could you be a moviemaker? Perhaps. Finish these lines of dialogue with unexpected phrases to get some ideas for your script.

I thought I told you to ____ .

I don't understand why you ____ .

Do you think we could ____ together?

Lesson Two

Read about it

- What does the title of the film mean?
- How do the titles of the reviews give you a hint of each one's tone?

Two Reviews:
Crouching Tiger, Hidden Dragon

Ang Lee directing *Crouching Tiger, Hidden Dragon*

Film reviews are subjective and often vary, giving different points of view on the same film based on the critic's personal preferences. Compare these two reviews and decide if you would want to see the movie.

Review 1:

An Epic of Romance and Martial Arts

When Ang Lee was growing up in Taiwan, most of the movies he watched were martial arts films. He had always wanted to direct one himself and finally got his chance with *Crouching Tiger, Hidden Dragon* (2000).

The movie takes its title from an old Chinese myth and refers to holding back your strength until the moment you need to attack. The story, however, is not so old. It was written as the fourth book in a series of five novels by Wang Du Lu (1909–1977), a self-taught author who wrote more than thirty novels but stopped writing in 1949 to work as a school teacher. Ang Lee may make movies from other novels in the series.

Crouching Tiger, Hidden Dragon is an epic tale in the form of a historical romance combined with martial arts, set in the nineteenth century. It tells the story of Jen (Zhang Ziyi), the young and beautiful daughter of a high official. Jen struggles against the two heroes of the tale, Li Mu Bai (Chow Yun-Fat) and his beloved, Yu Shu Lien (Michelle Yeoh). The heroes both seek revenge on Jade Fox, a murderous sorceress, and, at the same time, attempt to retrieve a magical sword.

The main "character" of the movie is China itself. The beautiful landscapes are a perfect backdrop to the music by composer Tan Dun, including solo cello parts played by Yo Yo Ma. On these landscapes, the characters engage in one of the main attractions of the movies, fight sequences carefully choreographed to look more like dance than fighting.

This is probably one of the best movies you will see this year, so go see it so you can return to see it again.

Review 2:
Crouching Tiger, Hidden Dragon
Ang Lee has said the title of his film, *Crouching Tiger, Hidden Dragon* (2000), refers to something that is hidden in each person. What's really hidden in this movie is any kind of story that makes sense. The basic plot involves several superhero-like characters each with an "I'm very calm, but don't make me mad!" attitude. All of them have serious trouble communicating with other human beings—other than by beating them up.

At the start of the movie, Li Mu Bai (Chow Yun-Fat) has dropped out of a monastery and goes to see his girlfriend, Yu Shu Lien (Michelle Yeoh). However, they can't have a normal relationship because of a feeble "Oh, you were my dead best friend's girlfriend so I can't love you" thing. Still, their lives keep getting tangled up, first over a stolen sword and then pursuing an evil elderly woman, Jade Fox, who looks like someone's grandmother. And like everyone else in the film, granny is a kung-fu expert.

But not just the usual kind of kung-fu expert—by hanging everyone on wires throughout much of the film and using the fast forward button on the movie camera, Ang Lee has made sure that all the fighting completely

A gravity-defying scene from *Crouching Tiger, Hidden Dragon*

ignores the laws of physics. This is particularly true for the frail Jen (Zhang Ziyi), 95 who looks like she'd have enough trouble carrying her groceries home from the supermarket let alone defeating gangs of dull-witted bad guys. If you fall asleep during the movie, you may wake up confused as there 100 are long sections where she remembers life with the kidnapper she should have married.

This is probably one of the worst movies anyone will see this year, so save yourself the bother and rent a Bruce Lee kung-fu DVD instead. 105

(636 words)

Vocabulary notes

1. **backdrop** (noun) the scenery behind something that you are looking at
2. **choreograph** (verb) to arrange how dancers should move during a performance
3. **epic** (adjective) an epic book, poem, or film tells a long story about brave actions and exciting events
4. **feeble** (adjective) not very good or effective
5. **frail** (adjective) someone who is frail is weak and thin because they are old or ill
6. **kidnap** (verb) to take someone somewhere illegally by force, often in order to get money for returning them
7. **martial art** (noun) a sport such as judo or karate, in which you fight with your hands and feet. Martial arts were developed in Eastern Asia.
8. **sorceress** (noun) a woman in stories who uses magic and receives help from evil forces
9. **tangled up** (adjective) to become twisted together, or make something become twisted together, in an untidy mess

Reading strategy

Reviews tell you a lot about the people who write them. After you read a review, try to describe the writer. Is he or she: kind, angry, intelligent, humorous, satirical, insulting?

Read and listen again to practice your pronunciation.

Discussion

After you read

A. Summarize the main idea in one sentence.

Fifty years ago, a movie was released and that was the final version. But now the future of movies is in question because of several advances in technology, and the unwillingness of movie companies to spend so much money and follow an artistic vision. So-called "director's cut" refers to movies that have scenes rearranged and restored and other parts cut out. Probably this is mostly just a way to increase sales. But DVD technology has allowed some filmmakers to add multiple endings. For example, initial audiences found the ending of the horror movie *28 Days Later* too depressing so the director added a happier ending. These, as well as a third ending, are all available on the DVD. Soon we may find ourselves watching a movie where we need to decide on every scene; everyone who watches it may become a director.

Culture note

What is the leading country for movies? India; more movies are made there each year than anywhere else.

B. Vocabulary check: Fill in the crossword.

Across
2. out of the ordinary
4. the written form of a movie
7. at peace
8. _____ -over commentary
9. togetherness of mouth and voice
10. a witch

Down
1. Orlando Bloom is the _____ of *The Lord of the Rings*
2. a long story
3. poor or ineffective
5. a three-part story
6. setting

C. Choose the best answer.

1. Ang Lee ___ .
   a. lives in Hollywood
   b. makes just one kind of film
   c. works in just one language
   d. directs movies

2. One can infer that Spike Lee is ___ .
   a. an actor
   b. a professor
   c. a filmmaker
   d. a student

3. *Big break* means ___ .
   a. divorce
   b. big surprise
   c. break the routine
   d. big opportunity

4. Why did Lee call his films the "Father Knows Best" trilogy?
   a. Fathers are the central characters.
   b. The theme is great fathers.
   c. The films star wise fathers.
   d. Fathers know more than mothers.

5. A conflict not in *The Wedding Banquet* is a person fighting against ___ .
   a. another person
   b. nature
   c. society
   d. him/herself

6. A central theme of Ang Lee's movies is not ___ .
   a. the problems between generations
   b. the different and changing roles of a father
   c. the way that food brings people together
   d. the role of men as homemakers in the family unit

7. A *self-taught author* is one who ___ .
   a. didn't learn to write in school
   b. can't read or write at all
   c. only writes by himself alone
   d. teaches others about his own writing methods

8. Which is not a criticism of the second reviewer of *Crouching Tiger, Hidden Dragon*?
   a. There is no story.
   b. The setting is inappropriate.
   c. The characters have serious problems.
   d. The fighting is unrealistic.

Exam strategy

If you find a really difficult question, leave it until last. You will sometimes find that answering easier questions can give you ideas about one that at first looked difficult.

Debate

Take one side, add your own ideas and debate in pairs or groups.

For: Movies are becoming predictable and boring.	*Against:* Movies will always continue to entertain and amaze us.
Points:	*Points:*
• There are only a limited number of plots available.	• Movies let us learn something about ourselves by watching others.
• Many movies now are just about special effects.	• Movies deal with life's issues at a safe distance.
• Every movie, unlike life, has a happy ending.	• New technologies are always extending what can be seen on a movie screen.
• _____	• _____
• _____	• _____
• _____	• _____

Debate strategy

When you debate, try to use statistics—facts and figures—to counter your opponent's opinions.

Say:

• "You may not like the movie, but it won fourteen major awards, including ... ."
• "More than _____ million people have seen this movie ... ."

More ideas to debate

"No art passes our conscience in the way film does, and goes directly to our feelings, deep down into the dark rooms of our souls."
Ingmar Bergman (1918–) Film and theater director

"If you can't believe a little in what you see on the screen, it's not worth wasting your time on cinema."
Serge Daney (1844–1992) Film critic

"It's the movies that have really been running things in America ever since they were invented. They show you what to do, how to do it, when to do it, how to feel about it, and how to look how you feel about it. Everybody has their own America, and then they have the pieces of a fantasy America that they think is out there but they can't see."
Andy Warhol (1928–1997) Artist

"Pictures are for entertainment, messages should be delivered by Western Union."
Samuel Goldwyn (1882–1974) Film producer

"Drama is life with the dull bits cut out."
Alfred Hitchcock (1899–1980) Film director

Think about it

What criticism do you think Alfred Hitchcock was answering?

Learn more

Newspapers, magazines and the WWW are full of movie reviews. Find a review for a movie you've seen and report to your class whether or not you agree with it and why.

Look online

Check out the website at www.read-and-think.com for extra learning resources.

Add new words to your personal dictionary on page 176.

Epidemic!

Lesson One

Before you read

- What is an epidemic?
- How do epidemics spread?

What is happening in the picture?

In seventeenth-century Europe, the plague was a constant threat

Reading strategy

You can help
remember and
describe an image
if you know how it
was made. This
picture is a
woodcut, made
from carving lines
in a piece of wood,
rubbing it with ink
and pressing it
onto paper. How
are other images
created?

Listen

Read about it

- Listen for pairs of words that naturally go together.

The Black Death

Sometime during the 1330s, large numbers of people in China began getting sick and dying from a new and mysterious disease. The symptoms included black swellings, or buboes, that appeared on a victim's neck, armpits or groin.

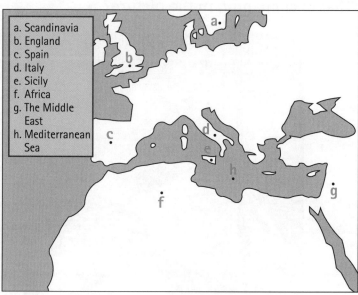

a. Scandinavia
b. England
c. Spain
d. Italy
e. Sicily
f. Africa
g. The Middle East
h. Mediterranean Sea

The plague spread throughout fourteenth-century Europe

Once they appeared, most people had less than a week to live. At this time, China was one of the world's busiest trading nations and, before long, the disease spread along its sea and land trade routes. One such trading route was overland to the Black Sea, where ships of many European nations came to exchange their goods for Chinese silks and other valuables.

In October of 1347, several of these ships, owned by Italian merchants, sailed home from the Black Sea, and entered the port of Sicily. By this time, many of the sailors and merchants on board had already contracted the disease and were dying. From the docks, it only took a few days for the disease to spread first to the town and then to the surrounding countryside.

The people of the town finally realized that the problem was more than just a few sick sailors; death itself had come on the ships. Records of the time showed that social order quickly broke down with parents unwilling to take care of sick children, servants fleeing and bodies left dead in houses where they fell, the stench telling the story of another family dead from the disease. In some cases, the disease came suddenly, with only a few hours between first feeling ill and death. The Italian writer Giovanni Boccaccio (1313–1375) noted that the disease's victims often "... ate lunch with their friends and dinner with their ancestors ... ."

Diseases come and go, but a disease that spreads in such a quick and contagious manner, infecting and killing in such numbers is called a *plague*. Just as it had spread by land and sea to Italy, the plague continued to spread to other parts of the known world. By the following August, it had spread as far north as Scandinavia and England, where it took on the name *The Black Death* because of its characteristic black tumors. Doctors—real and fraudulent—did everything they could to preserve the living and save the sick and dying but nothing worked. If they did not understand the cause, they could not think of a cure.

In the winter that followed, the plague seemed to disappear. At a time of great religious belief in Europe, people thought their prayers to God had been answered. But, as the weather warmed, the plague returned again and again with full strength for five years before it inexplicably disappeared. Between 1347 and 1352, 25 million people died: one third of Europe's population. But the plague had not left completely and isolated outbreaks continued until the 1600s.

The impact on society was enormous. Gangs of thieves took over the properties of the dead and terrorized the living. And with so many dead, there were hardly enough people to do all the work. By the end of the 1300s, those peasants who were left alive rebelled against their rulers, wanting more pay for their work. Similar revolts occurred in philosophy. People who felt God had not helped them during the plague began, for the first time, to question religious ideas.

Reading strategy

When portions of numbers are given as examples, do the math in your head to get the fuller picture and add to your knowledge. If *25 million people* was *one third* of Europe's population, what was Europe's total population?

And what caused all this death and change? The main culprit was a flea—a tiny flea that carried the disease and rode on rats that infested fourteenth century ships and towns. When the flea jumped to a human, one bite was enough to give someone the plague. Another form of the plague was spread by breathing the air of someone who had the disease. A third form was spread by the blood of an infected person. We understand these things now but, at the time, it must have seemed like the end of the world.

(646 words)

Reading strategy

Numbered points are not always identified when you see a word such as *third* on its own, go back and review the other points.

60

Vocabulary notes

1. **ancestor** (noun) a member of your family who lived a long time ago
2. **contagious** (adjective) a disease that is contagious can be passed from person to person by touch
3. **contract** (verb) to get an illness
4. **culprit** (noun) the person who is guilty of a crime or doing something wrong
5. **fraudulent** (adjective) intended to deceive people in an illegal way, in order to gain money, power, etc.
6. **inexplicably** (adverb) in the way that is too unusual or strange to be explained or understood
7. **infest** (verb) if insects, rats, etc., infest a place, there are a lot of them and they usually cause damage
8. **plague** (noun) a disease that causes death and spreads quickly to a large number of people
9. **tumor** (noun) a mass of diseased cells in your body that have divided and increased too quickly

Add new words to your personal dictionary on page 176.

Read and listen again to practice your pronunciation.

After you read

A. Answer these questions.

1. Where did the Black Death originate?
2. Who brought it to Europe?
3. What insect was responsible for the spread of the disease?
4. Why were doctors unable to cure the disease?
5. Is it likely the disease would spread in the same way today? Why or why not?

Understand what you read

Collocations

A collocation is a combination of two or more words that are commonly used together. Native speakers learn collocations naturally and use them without thinking, simply because they sound more natural. Synonyms cannot usually be substituted in collocations.

- *a strong drink*, but not *a powerful drink*
- *a powerful car*, but not *a strong car*

Here are four tips for working with collocations:
- Collocations have to be memorized.
- Many collocations work similarly between opposites, for example, *high/low energy, pressure, price, quality* and *light/heavy smoker, drinker, weight*.
- Breaking collocations and using odd words is sometimes done for effect or humor.
- If you fail to use the right collocation when you are speaking or writing, you will probably still be understood.

B. Complete the collocations with heavy or strong.

1. _____ snow

2. _____ smoker

3. _____ smell

4. _____ feeling

5. _____ traffic

6. _____ taste

7. _____ opinion

8. _____ sleeper

C. Number the sentences.

___ After ten days of ten themes, 100 stories have been told.

___ At the villa, they decide to entertain each other telling stories.

___ Each person has a day in charge of the theme of the stories.

_1_ Giovanni Boccaccio finished *Decameron* in 1353.

___ The book begins with a graphic description of the plague before introducing the reader to a group of young men and a group of young ladies.

___ The themes include deception, fortune, love and wit.

___ These ten Italians have escaped the plague by going to a villa in the hills near Naples.

D. Fill in the missing words. Use the correct form of the word.

- **alert** (noun) a warning to be ready for possible danger
- **contain** (verb) to stop something from spreading or escaping
- **outbreak** (noun) if there is an outbreak of fighting or disease in an area, it suddenly starts to happen
- **respiratory** (adjective) relating to breathing or your lungs
- **viral** (adjective) relating to or caused by a virus

What is SARS? Severe Acute _____ Syndrome is a _____ respiratory illness that was first reported in Asia in February 2003. In early March, the World Health Organization (WHO) issued a global _____ about SARS. Over the next few months, the illness spread to more than two dozen countries in North America, South America, Europe and Asia. By late July, however, no new cases were being reported and the illness was considered _____ . According to the WHO, 8,098 people worldwide became sick with SARS during this _____ ; of these, 774 died. For more information, check the WHO SARS website or visit the Centers for Disease Control and Prevention SARS website.

Source: Centers for Disease Control and Prevention, www.cdc.gov

What else do you know about SARS and similar viruses?

What about you?

New epidemics occur all the time. What would you do—and what would you tell others to do—during an epidemic?

Language note

A *syndrome* refers to a group of symptoms, especially when the cause or central reason is not known. It's often applied to diseases.

Lesson Two

- What is influenza?
- How many people died from Spanish Influenza?

The Spanish Flu

On the morning of March 11, 1918, at a military base in Kansas in the United States, one of the cooks felt sick and went to see the doctor. The doctor found that the cook's symptoms were typical of a common flu: he had a low fever, a slightly sore throat, a headache and his muscles were sore. The cook was told to rest in bed but, by noon, 107 other people at the camp were sick. Within two days, 522 people were sick, many with severe pneumonia.

Authorities might have hoped that the flu was simply a temporary and local problem. It was not. Soon other American military bases and ships began reporting similar widespread infections. Within seven days, it had spread right across the United States. Of all the ways a disease could spread, this was the worst: by air. Early on, the American government should have done something to share what was happening first to its soldiers and then to the general population, but little was done

Volunteers with masks feed children whose families are sick with the flu, ca. 1918

to help the rest of the world prepare. Later, the Americans were heavily criticized.

From the U.S., the flu soon spread to Europe, infecting the French by the beginning of April, before moving on to other European countries. By the middle of April, the disease had spread to China and Japan, as well as other Asian countries. By May, infections were widespread in both Africa and South America. There was practically no place in the world where anyone could escape the flu. Even remote Inuit populations, such as one in Nome, Alaska, suffered a 60 percent death rate. In other remote areas, the infections had a double burden, as there were not enough doctors or unaffected people to help. In Samoa,

Boys wear bags of camphor around their necks in the hopes of escaping the flu

for example, between 80 and 90 percent of the population was infected, but even those who survived died for other reasons, such as starvation, because they were too weak to gather and prepare food.

Not even the rich were safe from the disease. Millionaires, thinking that the sea air would be healthier, boarded ships to cross the Atlantic Ocean, but an average of 7 percent of the passengers died before the ship

Baseball player wears mask during the epidemic

reached the next port. A ship, with its confined space, was a perfect place for the disease to spread.

Laws were quickly passed to try to stop the spread of the disease. For example, stores in some countries were not allowed to hold sales to stop crowds gathering and spreading the flu even further, and medical certificates were required for travelers. Funerals were kept short to minimize the time people spent together. Just as had been the case during The Black Death, there were not enough coffins or grave diggers to bury all the dead.

Ironically, although the disease seems to have begun there, the U.S. was one of the least affected places, with somewhere between a total of 675,000 and 850,000 people dying. Elsewhere, the percentages of populations killed were much higher, such as in Spain, which had the dishonor of giving its name to the disease, Spanish Influenza. In all, a fifth of the world's population was infected and somewhere between 20 and 40 million people died. The true figure will never be known but some estimates put the figure as high as 80 million.

The only consolation was that the disease seemed to peak two to three weeks after arriving at a place and then not appear again. Eighteen months after the disease appeared, Spanish Influenza disappeared and has not been seen since.

At the time, scientists were without the proper tools to study the disease but, in 1997, preserved portions of a soldier's lung who had died on September 26, 1918, were discovered. From the dead tissue, scientists were able to learn something about the Spanish Flu.

It appears that the virus passed from birds to pigs, and then to humans. These types of viruses are particularly deadly because a pig's anatomy is so similar to a human's. As a pig's immune system tries to battle a new virus, the virus mutates into something stronger. When it finally leaps to humans, it can easily start an epidemic.

Could it happen again? Yes. With our extensive network of air travel, it might be worse, spreading a new disease around the world in days instead of months.

(721 words)

Reading strategy

When you make notes on what you read, group concepts together and write about their differences, for example, *plague*, *epidemic*, *virus* and *disease*.

Vocabulary notes

1. **burden** (noun) something difficult or worrying that you are responsible for
2. **dishonor** (noun) loss of respect from other people
3. **epidemic** (noun) a large number of cases of a disease that happen at the same time
4. **immune system** (noun) the system by which your body protects itself against disease
5. **infection** (noun) a disease that affects a particular part of your body and is caused by bacteria or a virus
6. **Inuit** (noun) someone who belongs to a race of people who live in the very cold northern areas of North America
7. **medical certificate** (noun) an official piece of paper signed by a doctor saying that you are too ill to work or that you are completely healthy
8. **mutate** (verb) if an animal or plant mutates, it becomes different from others of the same kind, because of a change in its genetic structure
9. **pneumonia** (noun) a serious illness that affects your lungs and makes it difficult for you to breathe
10. **virus** (noun) a very small living thing that causes infectious illnesses

Read and listen again to practice your pronunciation.

136

After you read

A. Summarize the main idea in one sentence.

A worldwide public health crisis is the abuse of antibiotics. One form of this abuse is when antibiotics are prescribed by doctors to help kill viruses. However, antibiotics are only effective against bacteria. By over-prescribing antibiotics, the bacteria can mutate into something stronger. The result is that some bacteria can no longer be treated by antibiotics.

B. Vocabulary check: Fill in the missing letters.

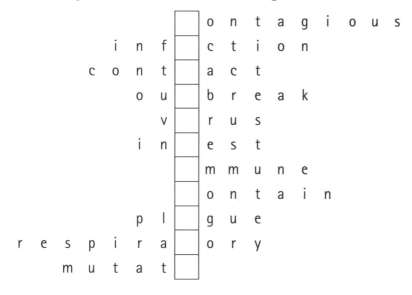

```
                        [ ] o n t a g i o u s
            i n f       [ ] c t i o n
      c o n t           [ ] a c t
            o u         [ ] b r e a k
            v           [ ] r u s
            i n         [ ] e s t
                        [ ] m m u n e
                        [ ] o n t a i n
            p l         [ ] g u e
  r e s p i r a         [ ] o r y
    m u t a t           [ ]
```

> ### Culture note
>
> During the 1918 Spanish Flu epidemic, children invented a macabre playtime rhyme:
> *I had a little bird,*
> *Its name was Enza.*
> *I opened the window,*
> *And in-flu-enza.*

C. Choose the best answer.

1. The Black Death originated in
   ___ .
   a. China
   b. Italy
   c. the Black Sea
   d. Sicily

2. Two features of the plague were
   that ___ .
   a. it was quick and contagious
   b. it only occurred in Italy
   c. it was real and fraudulent
   d. it spread by rabbits

3. Why were doctors of no help
   with the plague?
   a. Doctors didn't have medicines
      available.
   b. Doctors did not understand the
      cause.
   c. People died too quickly.
   d. The plague was too strong.

4. Which is not a result of the
   plague?
   a. Thieves took the property of the
      dead.
   b. There were not enough people
      to work.
   c. People questioned God.
   d. There was more travel by land
      and sea.

5. Which was not a way to catch
   the plague?
   a. A flea bite
   b. Infected air
   c. Infected blood
   d. Infected food

6. Which was not a symptom of
   the Spanish Flu?
   a. Low fever
   b. Slightly sore throat
   c. Sneezing
   d. Headache and sore muscles

7. The Americans were heavily
   criticized because ___ .
   a. they didn't help people in
      remote places
   b. they didn't tell others of the
      sickness
   c. they started the epidemic
   d. they spread the flu to Europe

8. Which statement is not true?
   Some people faced further
   problems because ___ .
   a. they lived in remote areas
   b. there weren't enough doctors
   c. there were few infected people
      to help the sick
   d. there was not enough food.

Debate

Take one side, add your own ideas and debate in pairs or groups.

For: We are in danger of another global epidemic.

Points:
- An epidemic is always a surprise.

- Many new diseases are resistant to antibiotics.

- Many parts of the world are over-populated and susceptible to disease.

- _____

- _____

- _____

Against: We are prepared for a global epidemic.

Points:
- People know what to expect because of previous epidemics.

- International communication is much better now.

- Scientists can create cures faster than before.

- _____

- _____

- _____

Debate strategy

When you debate, prepare historical examples to make your arguments stronger.

Say:
- "Something quite similar happened in ... ."
- "There is little difference between now and ... ."

Sometimes it's good to give historical examples and challenge your opponent at the same time.

Say:
- "Have you forgotten ...?"

Another idea to debate

"Neither physicians nor medicines were effective. Whether because these illnesses were previously unknown or because physicians had not previously studied them, there seemed to be no cure. There was such a fear that no one seemed to know what to do. When it took hold in a house it often happened that no one remained who had not died. And it was not just that men and women died, but even sentient animals died. Dogs, cats, chickens, oxen, donkeys, sheep showed the same symptoms and died of the same disease. And almost none, or very few, who showed these symptoms, were cured. The symptoms were the following: a bubo in the groin, where the thigh meets the trunk; or a small swelling under the armpit; sudden fever; spitting blood and saliva (and no one who spat blood survived it). It was such a frightful thing that when it got into a house, as was said, no one remained. Frightened people abandoned the house and fled to another."

Marchione di Coppo Stefani (1336–?) Italian writer

Learn more

How many people in your country get the flu each year? Use the library and the WWW to find facts and figures about viruses and epidemics in your country and report them to your class.

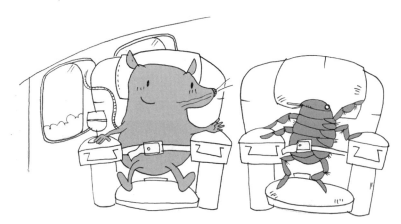

Look online

Check out the website at www.read-and-think.com for extra learning resources.

Add new words to your personal dictionary on page 176.

The Tale of Genji

Lesson One

Before you read

- Who was Murasaki Shikibu?
- When was the first novel written?

What is happening in the picture?

Prince Genji with a concubine

Read about it

- Listen for sentences that repeat certain sounds two or more times.

The World's First Novelist

Among the most remarkable of Japan's achievements is the creation of the world's first novel, *The Tale of Genji*, more than a thousand years ago and hundreds of years before anything similar was written elsewhere. For some, it is even more amazing that this novel was written not by a man, but by a woman. Murasaki Shikibu (973–1025?) wrote her novel at a period of Japanese history when few females were educated.

The Heian Period (794–1192) was an important phase in Japanese history because of the enduring peace and prosperity enjoyed under the ruling Fujiwara family. The Fujiwara clan moved the capital from Nara—away from the power struggles of the local Buddhist sect—to modern-day Kyoto, which they gave the name *Heian-kyo*, meaning *capital city of peace and tranquility*. Three centuries of peace allowed Japanese culture to develop and flourish in new and exciting ways, separate from the Chinese traditions they had followed for so long.

One of the first of these developments was a new system of writing that better reflected Japanese experience and attitudes. A court culture also developed around concepts of behavior, simplicity and sensitivity. At the forefront of these developments were the Heian court women, including Murasaki Shikibu, also known as *Lady Murasaki*.

Murasaki was a member of the important Fujiwara clan, and her father was not only a provincial governor, but also an important scholar. He longed for his son to follow in his footsteps but found that his daughter was much smarter than his son. He was said to have exclaimed, "If only you were a boy, how

Language note

Sometimes birth or death dates are unknown or not known for certain, especially for those born poor. In other cases, well-known people disappear from records before they die. A question mark is inserted to show this uncertainty.

happy I should be!" However, breaking with tradition, he allowed his daughter
25 to be educated in the Chinese classics.

Her home life in such an intellectually-stimulating atmosphere was probably
wonderful for young Murasaki, but it could not go on forever. Sometime in her
late teens or early twenties, a happy marriage was arranged for her to a distant
relative. In the year 999, she gave birth to her only child, a daughter. Two years
30 later, her husband suddenly died during a plague.

Fortunately for both Murasaki and all those who have enjoyed her writings for

almost a thousand
years, she did not fade
away to the life of a
35 lonely widow at this
point. Instead, through
her father's influence,
she was invited to join
the imperial court, as a
40 lady-in-waiting, a kind
of assistant and friend
to a noble person. She
was not immediately
popular and found the
45 court full of frivolous
fools. In the diary she

Heian Shrine, Kyoto

kept for two years at court, she described herself in this way:

"Pretty and bashful, disappearing from view, unsociable and proud, fond of
old stories and so preoccupied with poetry that others hardly exist, cruelly
50 looking down on the whole world ... this is the unpleasant opinion that people
have of me. Yet, when they come to know me, they say that I am oddly gentle,
quite unlike what they'd been led to believe. I know people are condescending
toward me, as if I were something cast away, but I have become used to it all
and say to myself, 'This is the way I am.'"

144

Murasaki's serious nature attracted the Empress Akiko, who had grown tired of the usual silly ladies-in-waiting. Murasaki became her favorite and secretly used her knowledge of Chinese to entertain the empress, first reading her Chinese stories and poetry and then even teaching her to read. As the available stories became too familiar, the empress encouraged Murasaki to write new ones. The result was the first novel, *The Tale of Genji*, which she may have begun before she came to court, but which she expanded using her keen observations of court customs and scandals.

Court records of the names of ladies-in-waiting show that sometime between 1025 and 1031, Murasaki left the court. She may have retired around age fifty to a Buddhist convent. Where and when she died is a mystery.

(659 words)

55

60

65

Reading strategy

Conjecture refers to guesses. In talking about things and events long gone, authors often use words such as *probably*, *possibly*, *might have* and *may have*. Be alert to these to decide what is a fact and what is a guess.

Vocabulary notes

1. **concept** (noun) an idea of how something is, or how something should be done
2. **condescend** (verb) to behave as if you think you are better, more intelligent, or more important than other people—used to show disapproval
3. **court** (noun) the place where a king or queen lives and works
4. **enduring** (adjective) continuing for a very long time
5. **be at the forefront (of sth)** (phrase) to be in a leading position in an important activity that is trying to achieve something or develop new ideas
6. **frivolous** (adjective) not serious or sensible, especially in a way that is not suitable for a particular occasion
7. **noble** (adjective) morally good or generous in a way that is admired
8. **observation** (noun) the process of watching something or someone carefully for a period of time
9. **sect** (noun) a group of people with their own particular set of beliefs and practices, especially within or separated from a larger religious group
10. **tranquility** (noun) pleasantly calm, quiet and peaceful

Add new words to your personal dictionary on page 176.

Read and listen again to practice your pronunciation.

145

After you read

A. Answer these questions.

1. Why was it unusual in the Heian Period for a woman to write?
2. What was a lady-in-waiting?
3. What qualities helped Murasaki write her novel?
4. What was the subject of *The Tale of Genji*?
5. What happened to Murasaki after she wrote her novel?

Understand what you read

Alliteration

Alliteration refers to the technique of repeating sounds at the beginning of words. Alliteration is used extensively in both poetry and novels.
Alliteration is used to:

- add rhythm
- establish a mood
- emphasize important words

Percy Shelley's (1792–1822) poem *England, in 1819* about King George III (1760–1820), who went permanently mad in 1810, uses alliteration with the letter *d*, and begins with these lines:

An old, mad, blind, despised, and dying king—
Princes, the dregs of their dull race, who flow
Through public scorn—mud from a muddy spring

Here are four tips for working with alliteration:

- The sounds, not the letters are important, for example, *eight* and *ache* are alliterative but *keen* and *knight* are not.
- Too much alliteration, such as in every word in a sentence, is sometimes used for silly exaggeration or general humor.
- Alliteration is often used in descriptions, for example, *a wild wind*, *a babbling brook*.
- It is difficult to translate alliterative phrases from one language to another.

Reading strategy

Knowing terms such as *alliteration* can help you remember examples of what you read. When you find especially interesting alliteration, copy them in your notebook.

B. Add alliterative words to the sentences.

1. The _____ witch turned the _____ prince into a frog.

2. The raft slipped suddenly into the _____ river.

3. When he awoke, the giant _____ spider was spinning its

   _____ web.

4. Looking up at the _____ tree, he decided to turn back.

5. Falling _____ , he finally found his parachute strings.

C. Unscramble the sentences.

1. poetry plays Literature novels and stories short includes

2. all Not novels literature considered are

3. simply Some entertainment empty are

4. Literature purpose has serious entertainment beyond usually a

5. works Many of to literature try society change

D. Fill in the missing words. Use the correct form of the word.

- **attempt** (noun) an act of trying to do something, especially something difficult
- **critic** (noun) someone whose job is to make judgments about the good and bad qualities of art, music, films, etc.
- **interaction** (noun) the activity of talking to other people, working together with them, etc.
- **psychological** (adjective) relating to the way that your mind works and the way that this affects your behavior
- **significant** (adjective) having an important effect or influence, especially on what will happen in the future

Most _____ agree that the first _____

English novels appeared in the early eighteenth century, beginning with three

novels by Daniel Defoe: *Robinson Crusoe* (1719), *Moll Flanders* (1722) and *Roxana*

(1724). Earlier _____ at novels were made, but they were

mostly silly romantic stories or philosophical works. A novel is generally defined

as fiction of a hundred or so pages that shows a realistic world in which there

are interesting _____ and social _____ .

What about you?

The Tale of Genji is made up of dozens of love stories. It is difficult to write hundreds of pages but it's not difficult to write one short love story and then write dozens more. Could you write a novel this way? Start with what you see around you and then add your imagination.

The beautiful warrior princess sat at her desk holding her sword ... .

Lesson Two

Read about it

- Who is Genji?
- What is the theme of the novel?

The Many Loves of Genji

The first and still one of the greatest novels of all time, *The Tale of Genji,* begins with the emperor falling in love with one of his concubines who is of a lower social class than his other concubines and wives. They become inseparable. Their relationship upsets everyone else around them, and becomes worse when she gives the emperor a son, Genji. But after a time, she sickens. The emperor moves her rooms closer to his but she realizes the time to die is near and, without ceremony, leaves with her son to return to her home. Soon after, she dies, leaving the emperor inconsolable. He takes Genji into his court and has him educated. Eventually, he finds another of the women in his court to remind him of his lost love, but he always has a fondness for Genji.

Genji grows into an intelligent and talented young man, adept at poetry, music and other courtly arts. The emperor wisely sees that he might be seen as a threat to his eldest son, the crown prince. To save Genji, he has him join a non-royal clan.

A late-night meeting with Prince Genji

As Genji grows, he becomes uncommonly handsome and admired by all. However, a conflict in the novel is that he is still feared by the family of the crown prince. The novel begins with Genji's affairs with various women around the capital, his friendships and his arranged marriage to his best friend's sister who gives him a son. After, he adopts a young girl, Murasaki, who later becomes the love of his life. Murasaki's name was then used by the court ladies for the author herself.

Throughout the novel, the relationship Genji has with each woman is unique. In fact, one theme of the novel is the ever-changing nature of love. Genji experiences everything from longing for someone who does not love him in return to trying to avoid the advances of an elderly woman whom he detests. In this case, he has to use all his wits to escape with dignity.

Meanwhile, after his father, the emperor, dies, Genji's many love affairs become a source of scandal and he is forced to leave the capital. He visits temples and other towns and has various adventures on his travels. The details in the extensive descriptions in the novel

The ghost of Lady Yugao; she was killed by the jealous spirit of one of Genji's mistresses

have provided historians with a fuller picture of the Heian Period.

In time, Genji returns to the capital. He sets up house with Murasaki and several other ladies. An older and wiser Genji becomes more influential at court and his interests shift to finding ways to help the fortunes of his children and grandchildren.

In the last ten chapters of the novel, the focus returns to matters of love, and follows the quite different lives of Genji's son and grandson.

In terms of conflict, there is not one central idea governing the entire novel. Instead, there are a series of overlapping tales, each with its own conflict, as Genji explores life with three wives and countless mistresses he has met at court and on his travels. As the story progresses, the various conflicts complicate each other. Altogether, more than 400 distinct characters appear and reappear throughout seventy years. All are documented in fifty-four books or chapters, totaling more than one thousand pages in English.

As she wrote the novel, it was probably Murasaki's intention that it merely be read aloud. She could not have imagined it would have been so popular that people would still be reading it today. The original manuscripts were soon lost and the only records are from twelfth-century reproductions. From that time on, it became the custom for wealthy patrons to illustrate key scenes from the novel and add passages from the text. These were set onto scrolls together as illustrated books. Today, some of these scrolls are regarded as Japanese national treasures.

(641 words)

Vocabulary notes

1. **concubine** (noun) a woman in the past who lived with and had sex with a man who already had a wife or wives, but who was socially less important than the wives
2. **detest** (verb) to hate something or someone very much
3. **inconsolable** (adjective) so sad that it is impossible for anyone to comfort you
4. **mistress** (noun) a woman that a man has a sexual relationship with, even though he is married to someone else
5. **overlap** (verb) if two or more things overlap, part of one thing covers part of another thing
6. **patron** (noun) someone who supports the activities of an organization, for example by giving money
7. **unique** (adjective) unusually good and special

Reading strategy

When you read a novel, you often find autobiographical tales about the author. What things might you guess about the author, based on the plot of this novel?

Read and listen again to practice your pronunciation.

After you read

A. Summarize the main idea in one sentence.

"One day, the emperor noticed *The Tale of Genji* in the empress's rooms. He offered his usual petty insults and then handed me a poem to which he had attached a sprig of plum-blossom. The poem read, 'What with these ardent tales of love, little can I think that men have passed you by, as they might this plum-tree's sour fruit.' And so I replied, 'If no man has tasted, who can say if the fruit is sour, or if the writer of these tales herself has known such love?'"
From the diary of Murasaki Shikibu

B. Vocabulary check: Circle the words.

V	O	F	O	A	C	O	N	D	E	S	C	E	N	D	I	N	D
C	Q	W	O	R	D	H	M	J	C	O	N	C	U	B	I	N	E
J	G	Q	B	O	B	S	E	R	V	A	T	I	O	N	S	C	Z
I	N	C	O	N	S	O	L	A	B	L	E	U	S	D	Y	P	I
F	I	N	T	E	R	A	C	T	I	O	N	S	Z	E	J	S	P
O	V	E	R	L	A	P	P	I	S	G	C	U	E	T	C	Y	J
M	C	C	R	I	T	I	C	S	I	J	R	K	P	E	O	C	E
I	U	Y	V	S	H	Q	U	N	I	Q	U	E	S	S	U	H	X
S	S	C	K	I	P	Q	F	N	S	I	S	V	T	T	R	O	F
T	T	O	D	G	N	J	C	Z	S	E	C	T	P	D	T	L	R
R	O	N	N	A	T	T	E	M	P	T	S	A	J	E	O	I
E	M	C	T	I	C	D	D	M	R	O	E	I	T	O	N	G	V
S	E	E	N	F	O	R	E	F	R	O	N	T	R	A	D	I	O
S	X	P	O	I	S	N	T	F	V	M	U	R	O	O	U	C	L
X	R	T	B	C	B	O	E	E	R	X	O	A	N	E	R	A	O
I	A	S	L	A	T	B	Y	T	P	D	K	B	U	C	I	L	U
T	K	E	E	N	Z	F	G	W	F	N	V	N	C	F	N	M	S
D	U	D	R	T	R	A	N	Q	U	I	L	I	T	Y	G	T	B

attempt
concept
concubine
condescend
court
critic
detest
enduring
forefront
frivolous
inconsolable
interaction
mistress
noble
observation
overlap
patron
psychological
sect
significant
tranquility
unique

Reading strategy

An *abridgement* is a shorter version of a book. Abridgements are often offered for longer books, especially novels. Reading an abridgement can often help you understand the most important points of a novel.

152

C. Choose the best answer.

1. Which of the following did not develop and flourish during the Heian Period?
   a. A new system of writing
   b. Court culture
   c. The allowing of women into court
   d. Women's education

2. Murasaki's father was not ___ .
   a. a member of an important clan
   b. a provincial governor
   c. an important scholar
   d. a man-in-waiting

3. Murasaki cannot be described as ___ .
   a. serious
   b. intelligent
   c. gentle
   d. condescending

4. Murasaki's *The Tale of Genji* is based upon ___ .
   a. observations of court customs and scandals
   b. enduring peace and prosperity during the Heian Period
   c. Chinese Buddhist tradition
   d. marriage, motherhood and being a widow

5. A synonym for *adept* is ___ .
   a. performing
   b. able
   c. practiced
   d. enjoyed

6. A synonym for *lady-in-waiting* is ___ .
   a. assistant and friend
   b. governor and scholar
   c. noble person
   d. storyteller

7. Genji's parents' relationship upset everyone because ___ .
   a. his mother was from a lower class
   b. his father was very old
   c. his father already had many concubines
   d. his mother was sick

8. Genji was a threat to the crown prince because he might ___ .
   a. take the throne
   b. have a son and heir
   c. marry many women
   d. adopt young Murasaki

9. One theme of the novel is ___ .
   a. the nature of nature
   b. the loss of a wife
   c. the fear of family
   d. the difficulties of court

10. There are themes of conflict in *The Tale of Genji*. Which is not a conflict described by the author?
    a. Genji versus the royal family
    b. Men versus women
    c. Lower class versus upper class
    d. Modern versus traditional

Exam strategy

Don't let other students make you nervous before or during an exam. In the exam room, ignore students who write quickly or leave early.

Debate

Take one side, add your own ideas and debate in pairs or groups.

For: Novels are an important part of life.	*Against:* The novel is dead.
Points:	*Points:*
• Novels let us see the world in new ways.	• There are more novels published than anyone can ever hope to read.
• Novels teach us something new about ourselves.	• Many novels just repeat the same stories with new characters.
• New novels reflect the modern world.	• Reading novels is a waste of time.
• _____	• _____
• _____	• _____
• _____	• _____

Debate strategy

When you debate, try to avoid personal attacks. Instead of insulting your opponent or questioning their qualifications, address the debate topic. When someone attacks you, keep to the topic.

Say:
- "I can see you don't have enough ideas to support your point of view, but that's no reason to attack me."
- "Insulting me won't help your argument."
- "It would be better to stick to the points, if you have anything else to say about it."

More ideas to debate

"Writing novels preserves you in a state of innocence—a lot passes you by—simply because your attention is otherwise diverted."
Anita Brookner (1928–) Writer

"The unread story is not a story; it is little black marks on wood pulp. The reader reading it makes it live: a live thing, a story."
Ursula K. Le Guin (1929–) Writer

"A classic is something that everybody wants to have read and nobody wants to read."
Mark Twain (1835–1910) Writer

"A critic is a legless man who teaches running."
Anonymous

"A good novel tells us the truth about its hero; but a bad novel tells us the truth about its author."
G.K. Chesterton (1874–1936) Writer

"Either write something worth reading or do something worth writing."
Benjamin Franklin (1706–1790) Politician, inventor and writer

Reading strategy

The Benjamin Franklin quote makes use of a literary device called *chiasmus*, in which the order of the ideas in the first of two clauses is reversed in the second. Once you know the name of a term, it's easier to remember examples.

Learn more

Many classic novels can be read for free on the WWW. Look for an example and tell your class about the first chapter.

Look online

Check out the website at www.read–and–think.com for extra learning resources.

Add new words to your personal dictionary on page 176.

The Robots Are Coming!

Lesson One

Before you read

- What is a thinking machine?
- How will robots change our lives?

How does the movie compare to reality?

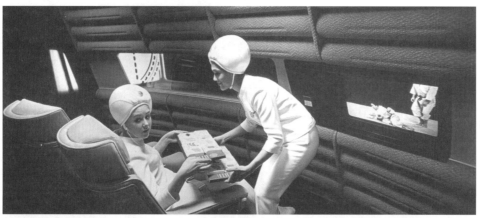

Flight attendants prepare to eat aboard a spaceship in the 1968 movie *2001: A Space Odyssey*

The reality of life in space

Reading strategy

Artists often try to predict the future, but looking at pictures of the future from long ago we see they seldom get it right. For example, most older pictures of the future do not show pollution.

• Listen for ways in which machines are given human qualities.

Killer Robots

Few people have ever heard of thirty-seven-year-old Kenji Urada. But while working at a manufacturing plant in 1981, 5 he had the dubious distinction of becoming the first person to be killed by a robot.

The idea of robots killing people has long been a fascination of 10 science fiction writers and scientists. When Urada died, people realized that the robot had broken the first of Isaac Asimov's (1920–1992) three robot laws:

15 1. A robot may not injure a human being or, through inaction, allow a human being to come to harm.

2. A robot must obey orders given it by human beings except where such orders would conflict with the first law.

3. A robot must protect its own existence as long as such protection does not 20 conflict with the first or second law.

Urada's death was an accident; he was trying to repair the manufacturing plant robot but didn't turn it off properly. The accident made people more aware of the dangers, and new rules were brought in to protect people. However, many people are still concerned about the impact of robotics and computing on their daily lives.

Humanoid robot

Robotic arm at a truck manufacturing plant

Movies and novels certainly haven't made people feel more comfortable. 25
Robots and computers are almost always depicted as evil geniuses that want
to destroy the world. One example is found in the novel and film *2001: A
Space Odyssey* by Sir Arthur C. Clarke (1917–), a scientist who first thought
of the idea for Earth's satellites. The story relates how a spaceship travels
on a mysterious search for alien signals coming from one of Jupiter's moons. 30
On board the spaceship is a supercomputer called HAL 9000.

HAL is responsible for running everything on the spaceship and speaks in a
normal calm voice but, as it becomes sentient, it decides to kill all the humans
on board. Essentially, the story is a metaphor of how we create a tool without
thinking that it might kill us one day. Other movies, such as the *Terminator* 35
series, use the same idea, but in this case a supercomputer has been put in
charge of the world's defenses and starts a nuclear war.

But how likely are such scenarios? Will robots and computers ever be able to
think? If so, will they have reason to kill humans one day?

By human standards, most robots and computers are incredibly stupid. Yes, 40
they might, like the supposedly brilliant IBM supercomputer "Deep Blue," be

able to win at chess, but this is only a trick of the computer's ability to calculate mathematical chance at lightning speed. If you asked the same computer why people play chess or if playing

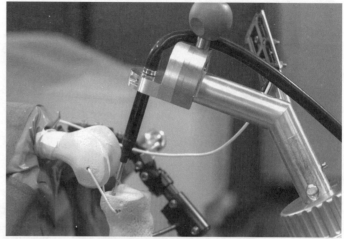

Test of a robotic arm designed to perform knee surgery

chess is fun, it might be able to find an answer that someone had told it, but it couldn't think of the answer on its own any more than an ant could.

But an ant is an interesting model. Ants are tiny and their brains are even tinier, but they still seem capable of organizing themselves to do complex activities. Artificial intelligence researchers have been looking at ants and other cooperative insects such as bees as models of machine intelligence. A lot of insect behavior, or even that of birds, often follows a few simple rules. For example, scientists studying bird behavior have created virtual birds on the computer that fly in formation. The rules they use to do this are:

- Don't go backward.
- Keep a meter away from other birds.
- Don't fly more than two meters away from other birds.
- Keep away from the ground and do not fly too high or too far.

What if machines could be programmed to do the same thing? Already, military organizations around the world are working on robots that could be used instead of human soldiers to fight in wars. The rules they would follow would be much more complex, but would involve recognizing friends from enemies.

As it has sometimes been difficult for human soldiers to recognize friends from enemies during battles, perhaps we should be very worried about giving robots the reasons and capacity to break Asimov's three laws.

(678 words)

Reading strategy

Bullet points are often used where there is no special order in a list and where one thing is no more important than another.

Vocabulary notes

1. **artificial intelligence** (noun) the study of how to make computers do intelligent things that people can do, such as think and make decisions
2. **capacity** (noun) someone's ability to do something
3. **distinction** (noun) the quality of being special in some way
4. **dubious** (adjective) a dubious honor, etc., is the opposite of an honor—used about something unpleasant that happens
5. **formation** (noun) the way in which a group of things are arranged to form a shape
6. **robotics** (noun) the study of how robots are made and used
7. **scenario** (noun) a situation that could possibly happen
8. **sentient** (adjective) able to experience things through your senses
9. **supercomputer** (noun) a computer that is more powerful than almost all other computers

Add new words to your personal dictionary on page 176.

Read and listen again to practice your pronunciation.

After you read

A. Answer these questions.

1. What did the computer in *2001: A Space Odyssey* try to do?
2. In what way is IBM's Big Blue not very smart?
3. How can ants be used as a model for an intelligent computer?
4. What is the basic idea behind Asimov's robot laws?
5. What is the metaphor in *2001: A Space Odyssey*?

Personification

Personification is a figure of speech that talks about an animal, object or idea as if it were human. Personification is mainly used to express a certain feeling or attitude toward something and to control the way a reader thinks about it. For example, a humming robot could be either *a stupidly humming robot or a happily humming robot.*

Here are four tips for working with personification:
- Personification is opinion; don't accept it as fact.
- Personification gives clues to the author's point of view.
- Personification is often used several times in a sentence or paragraph.
- Personification is common in fiction, but not in non-fiction writing.

B. Write descriptions of each thing to give it human qualities.

1. The car _____ .

2. The bird _____ .

3. The rain _____ .

4. The computer _____ .

5. The staircase _____ .

C. Number the sentences.

John Searle's Chinese Room

____ But someone outside the room only sees a question go in and sees an answer come out.

____ Imagine that an English-speaking person who doesn't understand Chinese is inside the room.

____ It looks like the person in the room understands Chinese, but he doesn't.

____ The man only needs to see the question and match it to one in the book.

____ The rule book explains how the Chinese characters should be organized.

____ Then he gives back the answer as a series of Chinese characters exactly as the book instructs.

____ With him in the room is an extremely thick rule book, written in English.

_1_ Philosopher John Searle (1932–) explains artificial intelligence by using the example of what he calls "The Chinese Room."

_9_ Like a computer, the man is just following rules.

D. Fill in the missing words. Use the correct form of the word.

- **competence** (noun) the ability to do something well
- **enrich** (verb) to improve the quality of something, especially by adding things to it
- **fruitful** (adjective) producing good results
- **micro–** (prefix) extremely small
- **mutually** (adverb) something that is mutually acceptable, etc., is acceptable, etc., to both or all the people involved

Several scientists have suggested that rather than create a robot that thinks like a person, it would be better to create one that thinks like something else.

Many scientists have long questioned the idea of creating a robot brain with the same level of _____ as a human brain. Instead, they think a more _____ approach might be to look at building a robot with one or more _____ skills. A bee, for example, has an extremely small brain but is able to do an amazing range of activities, including flying and finding its way home as well as gathering food. Part of a bee's success is that it is able to work with other bees in a _____ beneficial manner. Perhaps future robots will look less like metal people and more like small spiders, perhaps _____ with the ability to spin webs for our steel fences.

What animals and insects would be good models for a thinking computer?

What about you?
A *cyborg* is someone who is part human and part robot. In future many people may want to be cyborgs with robot eyes and ears to see and hear much better than any human. Would you want to add robot parts to make you faster, stronger and smarter?

Lesson Two

- What is the future of the human race?
- Will people be replaced by robots one day?

The Last Letter

June 1, 2050

Anyone
Anywhere

Dear Anyone,

As the last of the Homo sapiens on Earth—and an old human at that—I've 5
decided to write the last letter. Perhaps someone, somewhere, sometime will
be able to read it. Perhaps only robots and computers will peruse it and have a
good laugh. How did I come to be the last living person? Let me explain.

People have dreamed about robots and thinking machines for thousands of
years. The ancient Greeks talked about *Talos*, a giant metal robot that supposedly 10
walked around the island of Crete three times each day. It was a slave that
helped the King of Crete fight his enemies. And this has always been the
problem. People have always thought of robots as slaves; they never thought
these powerful tools might one day become the masters and make people the
slaves. 15

At first, people didn't think about how they were being surrounded by thinking
machines. But they were soon everywhere. Some of the earliest thinking
machines controlled the temperature—when it was too cold, they turned up

Culture note

With e-mail,
writing letters has
become less
common.
However, letters
are still best for
certain kinds of
messages, especially
letters of condolence
after someone has
become very sick
or died.

the heat and when it was too warm, they turned on the air conditioner. This doesn't sound too dangerous, but once people got used to temperatures and then lights being controlled, they started having machines control the doors of buildings, fire sprinklers and many household appliances. Robot vacuum cleaners started roaming around the inside of people's homes and machines programmed to tend the gardens worked outside. It was great! People had more free time! Well, actually, only rich people had more free time. The humans who used to do a lot of the robots' jobs had to find other work. Suddenly, the world was breaking into two classes: technology haves and technology have-nots.

Of course, it was only natural that the technology have-nots would want more. Soon, they started stealing from and rebelling against humans with technology. Something had to be done. Again, machines seemed to be the answer. People installed security systems in their homes and businesses. Computers used video cameras to watch everything and everyone. When security deteriorated, people started thinking about having robot guards. Of course, the robot guards were just supposed to stop and detain criminals, not hurt them. But when robot guards started being destroyed, people insisted that the robots be armed.

While all this was going on, two other lines of research were being pursued in artificial intelligence laboratories. One area of interest was robots that could recreate themselves. The plan was to send them to a new planet, like Mars, and let them start building cities for colonists who would come after. No one ever thought of what would happen if they escaped their labs on Earth. Another research direction was in parallel processing. Rather than just create a supercomputer, scientists realized that several ordinary computers networked together could think in the same way. Soon, computers connected over the Internet were talking to each other and solving problems. But they could also create problems.

One of the real problems was the whole idea of remote control. In Finland, people started using their mobile phones to control all kinds of things in their homes. They wanted their rooms warm when they got home from work and wanted the stoves cooking their dinners and the bathtubs full of hot water. But what if someone—or something—else could control these same things? What if your rooms could be turned ice cold while you slept, your oven set on fire and your bathtub made to overflow? When my old wind-up radio still worked, the first news reports blamed have-not computer hackers for spreading computer viruses that made robots and computers do everything they could to kill humans, starting with interrupting food, water, electricity and fuel supplies. I don't know if that's true. 55

But I did see the end coming. Forty years ago, I left the city, moved into a cave high in the mountains and started growing my own food and making everything I need by hand. When the first robot wars started, they didn't even notice I was up here, without electricity or a single machine. Eventually, of course, the robots ruled the world. And what did they need humans for? 60

Well, I better finish this now. The robot mailman will be here in a few minutes.

Yours sincerely and good luck,

Eve Last 65

(729 words)

Vocabulary notes

1. **arm** (verb) to provide weapons for yourself, an army, a country, etc., in order to prepare for a fight or a war
2. **cave** (noun) a large natural hole in the side of a cliff or hill, or under the ground
3. **colonist** (noun) someone who settles in a new colony
4. **detain** (verb) to officially prevent someone from leaving a place
5. **deteriorate** (verb) to become worse
6. **hacker** (noun) someone who secretly uses or changes the information in other people's computer systems
7. **have-not** (noun) the poor people in a country or society
8. **Homo sapien** (noun) the type of human being that exists now
9. **peruse** (verb) to read something, especially in a careful way
10. **sprinkler** (noun) a piece of equipment on a ceiling that scatters water if there is a fire

Reading strategy

Science fiction uses the future to talk about issues that are important today. Always look for the writer's message in a science fiction story.

Read and listen again to practice your pronunciation.

After you read

A. Summarize the main idea in one sentence.

Since people first lived in caves, we have always been afraid of something. First it was wild animals, but when wild animals were more easily hunted, people became afraid of other things. People need something to be afraid of and seemingly choose something new every few years. Right now the popular thing to be afraid of is computers, but soon everyone will be comfortable with them and the fear will shift to something else. Perhaps robots?

B. Vocabulary check: Fill in the crossword.

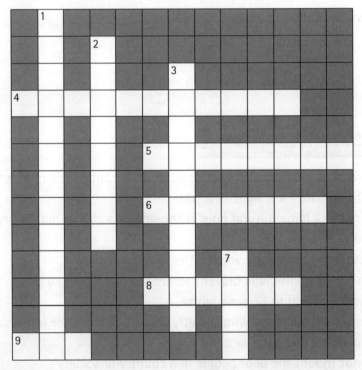

Across

4. to fall apart
5. an antonym of *native*
6. a poor person
8. to prevent someone from leaving
9. to provide weapons

Down

1. for example, IBM's Big Blue
2. a possible situation
3. a human being
7. a rock dwelling

C. Choose the best answer.

1. *Dubious distinction* means ___ .
   a. unsettled opinion
   b. suspect quality
   c. questionable honor
   d. uncertain nature

2. What is not one of Asimov's robot laws?
   a. A robot may not injure or harm a human being
   b. A robot must not come into conflict
   c. A robot must protect its own existence
   d. A robot must obey human orders

3. A synonym for *sentient* is ___ .
   a. emotional
   b. thinking
   c. angry
   d. human

4. People are less comfortable because robots and computers are depicted ___ .
   a. in a negative way
   b. as geniuses
   c. as world leaders
   d. as inconvenient

5. Sir Arthur C. Clarke is not ___ .
   a. a writer
   b. a scientist
   c. an inventor
   d. an astronaut

6. What is not a result of Urada's working on the plant robot?
   a. Death
   b. New rules
   c. Home robots
   d. Increased awareness

7. Which statement is not true? Computers can ___ .
   a. operate appliances
   b. play chess
   c. calculate chance
   d. think independently

8. Homo sapiens are ___ .
   a. humans
   b. the Earth
   c. robots
   d. computers

9. In the letter, ___ .
   a. everyone was safer
   b. some people became unemployed
   c. homes and gardens were tidier
   d. no one has any free time

10. Which is not an interest of computer research?
    a. Robots that can recreate themselves
    b. Parallel processing
    c. Artificial intelligence
    d. Ancient Roman computing

Exam strategy

After an exam, make notes on what topics or question types gave you the most problems. Use this information to help you study for your next exam.

Debate

Take one side, add your own ideas and debate in pairs or groups.

For: Computers and robots will one day be smarter than humans.
Points:
- A hundred years ago they were fantasy, but now they are common.

- Computers are improving every year.

- Computers have started designing computers.

- _____

- _____

- _____

Against: Computers and robots will never be smarter than humans.
Points:
- They are quite stupid.

- They don't work without electricity; we can just pull the plug.

- Computers only do what they're told.

- _____

- _____

- _____

Debate strategy

When you debate, be prepared to challenge idle speculation: opinions that are not backed up by facts.

Say:
- "Although it's nice to think that ... no one really knows what will happen."
- "If you are right, there must be some example from the past you can use as a comparison."
- "There's no point making predictions if you can't support them with evidence."

More ideas to debate

"The danger of the past was that men became slaves. The danger of the future is that men may become robots. True enough, robots do not rebel. But given man's nature, robots cannot live and remain sane."
Erich Fromm (1900–1980) Philosopher

"Do your duty and a little more and the future will take care of itself."
Andrew Carnegie (1835–1919) Industrialist and philanthropist

"There's a queasiness that people feel as they see the march of science into the brain and the mind, a fear that we'll be swallowed up and turned into robots."
Daniel Dennett (1942–) Professor and writer

"Any sufficiently advanced technology is indistinguishable from magic."
Arthur C. Clarke (1917–) Scientist and writer

> **Think about it**
>
> What does Arthur C. Clarke mean by *advanced technology* and *magic* appearing the same? Can you think of an example?

Learn more

What are the latest developments in artificial intelligence, computing and robotics? Look for articles on the WWW and report them to your class.

If you don't behave, the humans will get you!

Look online

Check out the website at www.read-and-think.com for extra learning resources.

Add new words to your personal dictionary on page 176.

Skills check

After finishing Unit 1, can you ...

☐ recognize some foreign words and the ways they are shown in sentences?

☐ talk about ideas of what makes a genius, using examples and arguments?

☐ remember and use new exam skills and reading strategies?

After finishing Unit 2, can you ...

☐ recognize explanations in context to find the meanings of new words?

☐ talk about different kinds of human rights and the language of legal documents?

☐ remember and use new exam skills and reading strategies?

After finishing Unit 3, can you ...

☐ read a biography to understand the key parts of a person's life—and guess what has been left out?

☐ talk about Jane Austen's life and some of the novels she wrote?

☐ remember and use new exam skills and reading strategies?

After finishing Unit 4, can you ...

☐ recognize and understand reported speech and how it is different from direct speech?

☐ talk about the history of chocolate and how calories and diets work?

☐ remember and use new exam skills and reading strategies?

After finishing Unit 5, can you ...

☐ understand some common idioms and recognize new idioms?

☐ talk about ghosts and whether they exist, as well as Lafcadio Hearn?

☐ remember and use new exam skills and reading strategies?

After finishing Unit 6, can you ...

☐ recognize and use similes that compare two things using *like* or *as*?

☐ talk about Marco Polo and his travels using arguments from different points of view?

☐ remember and use new exam skills and reading strategies?

After finishing Unit 7, can you ...

☐ recognize and use sequence phrases to understand a series of points?

☐ talk about the importance of labyrinths and mazes, explaining the differences and giving examples from a Greek myth?

☐ remember and use new exam skills and reading strategies?

After finishing Unit 8, can you ...

☐ make inferences and understand when the writer of a passage expects you to make inferences to understand hidden meanings?

☐ talk about the history of chess and the short story about computer games?

☐ remember and use new exam skills and reading strategies?

After finishing Unit 9, can you ...

☐ recognize different kinds of conflicts in fiction?

☐ talk about Ang Lee and some of his most famous movies, explaining their themes?

☐ remember and use new exam skills and reading strategies?

After finishing Unit 10, can you ...

☐ recognize and use collocations correctly?

☐ talk about famous plagues and epidemics in history and how they are caused and spread?

☐ remember and use new exam skills and reading strategies?

After finishing Unit 11, can you ...

☐ recognize and use alliteration correctly?

☐ talk about the first novelist and her famous novel?

☐ remember and use new exam skills and reading strategies?

After finishing Unit 12, can you ...

☐ recognize and use personification?

☐ talk about how robots and computers "think" and discuss future scenarios about how they might help or hurt us?

☐ remember and use new exam skills and reading strategies?

Exam strategies

1 In writing exams, don't try to make your writing too clever when you answer a question. Use direct simple sentences so you are sure the teacher knows what you mean.

2 In multiple choice questions, teachers sometimes use the same letter choice for two or three correct answers in a row just to confuse students. Don't think that every question must have a different letter from the previous one.

3 The order you choose to answer the questions doesn't matter; first answer the questions that are easiest for you. But mark the questions you haven't answered so you don't forget to go back to them.

4 In writing exams, take time to reread the question as you write to make sure you have not gone off the topic.

5 When studying for an exam, put yourself in the teacher's place and try to predict the questions that might be asked. And don't be afraid to ask a teacher before an exam what will be covered. It can't hurt to ask.

6 In multiple choice questions, some teachers take important or odd words from a reading and put them in the wrong answer. Think of what you know; don't be confused by what you don't know.

7 In writing exams, remember that longer is not always better. Answer the question; don't try to show everything you know.

8 When writing your answer, don't bother rewriting the question as part of your answer. It's a waste of time for you and the teacher. Just *answer* the question.

9 If you find a really difficult question, leave it until last. You will sometimes find that answering easier questions can give you ideas about one that at first looked difficult.

10 Write a practice exam with friends. Write some questions, set an alarm clock and see how well you do.

11 Don't let other students make you nervous before or during an exam. In the exam room, ignore students who write quickly or leave early.

12 After an exam, make notes on what topics or question types gave you the most problems. Use this information to help you study for your next exam.

Check your speed

Most of the readings in this book are around 600 words. Check how many words a minute you are reading and keep a record over the twenty-four main readings.

Minutes	1	2	3	4	5	6	7	8	9	10	11	12	13	14	15
600 words	600	300	200	150	120	100	86	75	67	60	55	50	46	43	40

Unit	1		2		3		4		5		6		7		8		9		10		11		12	
Lesson	1	2	1	2	1	2	1	2	1	2	1	2	1	2	1	2	1	2	1	2	1	2	1	2
Speed																								

Debate strategies

1   When you debate, start your argument by introducing your point of view and summarizing your main points. You can also summarize your opponent's reasons and examples, then present your own.

Say:
- "I believe that ... for three reasons."
- "She has said ... but the opposite is actually true for three reasons ... ."

2   When you debate, look for holes, or a lack of facts, in the other person's argument. Often people will try to sound like they know what they are talking about but don't have any supporting evidence.

Say:
- "While I agree with ... you don't have any facts to support ... ."
- "Your point about ... is correct, but you're very wrong about ... ."

3   When you debate, quote the other person's words to show that you understand what they are talking about. Then give your point of view.

Say:
- "You say that you believe ... but in fact ... ."
- "What you're trying to say is ... but the truth is ... ."

4   When you debate, don't be fooled by sweeping general statements. Ask for more information when the other person uses phrases such as, *hundreds of years* or *many countries.*

Say:
- "Excuse me, could you be more specific? Exactly how long was it?"
- "Excuse me, but that's too general. Please give me an example."

5   When you debate, pay attention if your opponent uses a country as an example. If they say, "In the United States ...," challenge him or her with the example of another country to throw the person off their argument.

Say:
- "Yes, well perhaps in the United States, but what about in (name of another country)?"
- "It may be true in the United States, but we're not in the U.S., are we?"

6   When you debate, make sure you agree exactly about the topic of the debate. Sometimes your opponent may try to change the topic to suit his or her examples.

Say:
- "Excuse me, you seem to be talking about another topic."
- "How does this relate to the topic of ...?"
- "Perhaps we are not discussing the same thing. I understand the topic is ... but you are talking about ... ."

7   When you debate, don't leave a question unanswered if you know the answer. If you don't know the answer, you can shift the topic.

Say:
- "That's an interesting question, but we are really talking about ... ."

8   When you debate, challenge the inferences your opponent makes. For example, if a person infers that you just don't understand, make it clear that you do.

Say:
- "My opponent is trying to infer that I don't understand, but I do. More importantly, she does not understand that ... ."

9 When you debate, try to use statistics—facts and figures—to counter your opponent's opinions.

Say:
- "You may not like the movie, but it won fourteen major awards, including ... ."
- "More than ___ million people have seen this movie ... ."

10 When you debate, prepare historical examples to make your arguments stronger.

Say:
- "Something quite similar happened in ... ."
- "There is little difference between now and ... ."

Sometimes it's good to give historical examples and challenge your opponent at the same time.

Say:
- "Have you forgotten ...?"

11 When you debate, try to avoid personal attacks. Instead of insulting the person you are talking to or questioning their qualifications, address the debate topic. When someone attacks you, keep to the topic.

Say:
- "I can see you don't have enough ideas to support your point of view, but that's no reason to attack me."
- "Insulting me won't help your argument."
- "It would be better to stick to the point, if you have anything else to say about it."

12 When you debate, be prepared to challenge idle speculation: opinions that are not backed up by facts.

Say:
- "Although it's nice to think that ... no one really knows what will happen."
- "If you are right, there must be some example from the past you can use as a comparison."
- "There's no point making predictions if you can't support them with evidence."

Personal dictionary

Use this page to keep a list of new words you discover in your reading. Write down the definitions if you need to, and then try to use each word in your writing and daily conversations in English.

_____   _____

_____   _____

_____   _____

_____   _____

_____   _____

_____   _____

_____   _____

_____   _____

_____   _____

_____   _____

_____   _____

_____   _____

_____   _____

_____   _____

_____   _____

_____   _____

_____   _____

_____   _____

Personal reading diary

Use this page to keep a list of what you read. As you read, try to answer these questions: What is the title? What is the genre (type of article, play or story)? What new vocabulary did I find? What strategies did I use to read it effectively? What did I learn from this? Did reading it change my mind in any way?

Title	Genre	Vocabulary	Strategies	I learned ...

Word list, by unit

Unit 1
abandon
accountant
apprentice
astounding
confine
downfall
excel
experiment
factor
gravity
innovate
invented
masterpiece
Nobel Prize
notary
proper
roam
shield
shyness
systematic
studio
technique
turning point

Unit 2
best interest
cannibal
capable
criticize
ethical
exotic
experiment
fundamental
inalienable
incite
omnivore
oppression
preamble
proclaim
respect
suffering
torture
tyranny
violate
whereas

Unit 3
ball
caprice
character

charades
draft
excitable
flatter
landowner
Michaelmas
minister
miserable
nerves
possession
preference
revise
sarcastic
satirical
scrupulous

Unit 4
allege
anxious
attach
cluster
consult
custom
execute
ghost story
haunt
invisibility
journalist
lining
merchant
ornament
paradoxically
prior
samurai
supernatural
volunteer

Unit 5
adore
all the rage
aristocracy
customer
emergence
excessuve
habit
introduce
monk
rage, be all the
ridiculous
reject
strenuous

technically
translate
vigorous

Unit 6
admit
appoint
calligraphy
carcass
catapult
deform
disturb
fallacious
historian
impress
imprison
monstrous
overlook
preposterous
presumably
romance
sew
snatch
supposedly
translate

Unit 7
allegory
astronomer
cathedral
dagger
diameter
dock
exit
labyrinth
lot
maze
mosaic
mourn
option
perish
passage
retrace
slay
unaware
victory

Unit 8
addiction
adventurous
bother

chance
constant
dice
dynamic
flair
gambling
guarantee
impractical
merge
notice
score
static
straw
tamper
twist

Unit 9
backdrop
bittersweet
choreograph
convention
epic
exceptional
feeble
frail
gay
generation
harmony
inadvertently
kidnap
martial art
script
sorceress
star
suspend disbelief
sync
tangled up
trilogy
voice-over

Unit 10
alert
ancestor
burden
contagious
contain
contract
culprit
dishonor
epidemic
fraudulent

immune system
inexplicable
infection
infest
Inuit
medical certificate
mutate
outbreak
plague
pneumonia
respiratory
tumor
viral
virus

Unit 11
attempt
concept
concubine
condescend
court
critic
detest
enduring
forefront
frivolous
inconsolable
interaction
mistress
noble
observation
overlap
patron
psychological
sect
significant
tranquility
unique

Unit 12
arm
artificial intelli-
gence
capacity
cave
colonist
competence
detain
deteriorate
distinction
dubious

enrich
formation
fruitful
hacker
have-not
Homo sapien
micro-
mutually
peruse
robotics
scenario
sentient
sprinkler
supercomputer

Word list, alphabetical

A
abandon
accountant
addiction
admit
adore
adventurous
alert
allege
allegory
all the rage
ancestor
anxious
appoint
apprentice
aristocracy
arm
artificial intelligence
astound
astronomer
attach
attempt

B
backdrop
ball
best interest
bittersweet
bother
burden

C
calligraphy
cannibal
capable
capacity
caprice
carcass
catapult
cathedral
cave
chance
character
charades
choreograph
cluster
colonist
competence
concept
concubine
condescend

confine
constant
consult
contagious
contain
contract
convention
court
critic
criticize
culprit
custom
customer

D
dagger
deform
detain
deteriorate
detest
diameter
dice
dishonor
distinction
disturb
dock
downfall
draft
dubious
dynamic

E
emergence
enduring
enrich
epic
epidemic
ethical
excel
exceptional
excessive
excitable
execute
exit
exotic
experiment
experimentation

F
factor
fallacious

feeble
flair
flatter
forefront
formation
frail
fraudulent
frivolous
fruitful
fundamental

G
gambling
gay
generation
ghost story
gravity
guarantee

H
habit
hacker
harmony
haunt
have-not
historian
Homo sapien

I
immune system
impractical
impress
imprison
inadvertently
inalienable
incite
inconsolable
inexplicable
infection
infest
innovate
interaction
introduce
Inuit
invent
invisibility

J
journalist

K
kidnap

L
labyrinth
landowner
lining
lot

M
martial art
masterpiece
maze
medical certificate
merchant
merge
Michaelmas
micro-
minister
miserable
mistress
monk
monstrous
mosaic
mourn
mutate
mutually

N
nerves
Nobel Prize
noble
notary
notice

O
observation
omnivore
oppression
option
ornament
outbreak
overlap
overlook

P
paradoxically
passage
patron
perish
peruse
piece
plague

pneumonia
possession
preamble
preference
preposterous
presumably
prior
proclaim
proper
psychological

R
rage, be all the
reject
respect
respiratory
retrace
revise
ridiculous
roam
robotics
romance

S
samurai
sarcastic
satirical
scenario
score
script
scrupulous
sect
sentient
sew
shield
shyness
significant
slay
snatch
sorceress
sprinkler
star
static
straw
strenuous
studio
suffering
supercomputer
supernatural
supposedly
suspend disbelief

sync
systematic

T
tamper
tangled up
technically
technique
torture
tranquility
translate
trilogy
tumor
turning point
twist
tyranny

U
unaware
unique

V
victory
vigorous
violate
viral
virus
voice-over
volunteer

W
whereas